First published by the Institute for Intuitive Intelligence in 2023
https://instituteforintuitiveintelligence.com/

Love Notes to the Divine:
On Becoming Spiritually Intimate

Ebook format: 978-0-6480950-8-8
Print: 978-0-6480950-7-1

Cover design by
Elise Elliott for Pass the Salt
www.passthesalt.com.au
Interior design by
Institute for Intuitive Intelligence
Author image by Chloe Horder
https://www.chloehorder.com/

LOVE NOTES TO THE DIVINE

On becoming spiritually intimate

Ricci-Jane Adams 2023

Dr. Ricci-Jane Adams is the principal of the Institute for Intuitive Intelligence®, a world-class, professional intuition training school. She trains exceptional spiritual people in the science and mysticism of Intuitive Intelligence®. The Institute leads the way in academic rigour, ethical grounding and social conscience, bringing a gold standard of professional excellence to an unregulated industry. Ricci-Jane is the author of the bestselling *Spiritually Fierce* and *Superconscious Intuition*. Ricci-Jane has a doctorate from the University of Melbourne in magical realism. She has devoted over twenty-five years to her spiritual awakening and is a qualified Transpersonal Counsellor.

Honestly, this book is dedicated, firstly to me. You did it, dear woman. You made it through the dark night. Celebrate all that you are! Next, to all those who kept their fierce gaze of love upon me, and never doubted me for a second.

CONTENTS

PROLOGUE

When I think about my legacy, the books I write mean the most to me. My soul is agitating me constantly towards writing. I have journaled since I was 16. I have two or three book ideas in my head at any given time. I have spent most of my life wishing I was a writer, and in my mid-forties, I finally recognise I always have been.

Writing moves me, rises me from my bed in the predawn darkness, fuels my fire, ignites my passion and excites me like nothing else. I follow that fierce joy now without question. I adore everything I do in my service, yet what I record in writing feels nearest to my soul's purpose. Before I created the Institute, I completed a doctorate in creative writing at the University of Melbourne and worked as an award-winning playwright with my plays produced worldwide.

When I left academia and theatre behind and gave everything to my soul path, my writing turned to the subject of intuition. But intuition has always been the gateway to intimacy with the divine. I have shared the short-form writings of this book previously, primarily on social media, and now they are collected here to offer a way home to Truth.

My service is my medicine, and the words written on these pages have supported me to stay on the path of non-dualism - the uncompromising path of reclaiming God-nature. This book could also be called Love Notes *From* the Divine, for I have received these words as instructions and consolations to my soul.

Remembering who we are in a noisy and demanding world can be challenging. These words are a balm to my soul, and I hope that is the same for you.

How to use this book

Love Notes to the Divine is a collection of contemplations and meditations to remind you who you are. The book is organised into the themes, ideas and values I share most about as a spiritual teacher. Each theme is a piece of the puzzle in increasing intimacy with our God nature.

You may read a passage each morning to inspire your daily devotion. You can read the book cover to cover. You can move through a particular theme that is resonating with you.

In what ever way you use these inspirations, give them space in your heart. Let the words alter you. They are direct reminders of who you are and invite you to a deep faith beyond the trinkets and superstitions of the new age. Let these words open the doors of perception and challenge any perceived limitations. You are fully human and fully divine, and this book shows you the way to live your holiness in a mundane world.

All my fiercest love,
Ricci-Jane

A note on pronouns

Love Notes to the Divine

As the principal of the Institute for Intuitive Intelligence, I have served women (including trans and femme-identifying) predominantly. This book uses feminine pronouns. The section on mysticism speaks mostly to women. After 5,000 years of patriarchy, it is a stark reality that women have a more difficult time accepting their intimacy with the divine and, in my experience, have benefitted from additional support to embody it. The rest of the themes speak to all, for indeed, beyond the polarity of male and female, we come home to Oneness. First, we must know how to honour what we are and to see no impediment because of our gender in embodying our holiness.

Shiva and Shakti. Masculine and feminine. Yin and yang. These polarities unite in God. Men and women carry both polarities within them, but history (and our present) has largely excluded women from feeling safe to be intimate with God as God. All of us benefit from correcting this error.

Ricci–Jane Adams

CONSCIOUSNESS

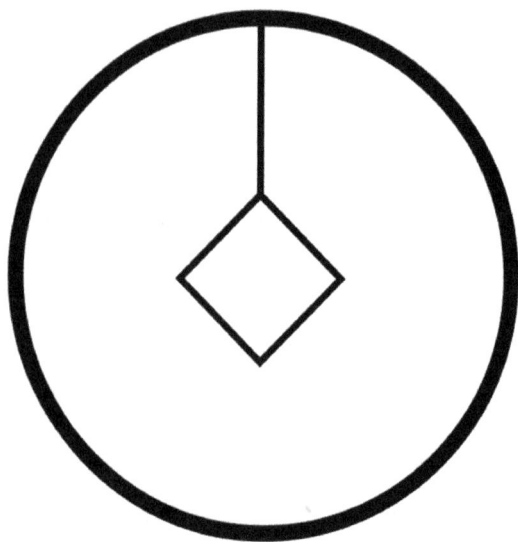

THE SOUL IS SINGULAR IN ITS PURPOSE: TO AWAKEN TO ITSELF AT DEEPER AND DEEPER LEVELS. WE COME INTO THIS CONSCIOUSNESS EXPERIMENT CALLED LIFE AND LAND ON EARTH SCHOOL TO FORGET SO WE CAN REMEMBER.

Every go-round that we have on Earth school, which is this local projection we're inhabiting and part of the consciousness experiment in which we are all participating, is an opportunity to deepen into our truth that we are God. We do this repeatedly until we finally break free of the habit of believing that we are single, finite, fragile, isolated humans with no capacity to change our lives. Until we meet ourselves as God, we will keep returning to the dream of Earth school.

APPROACH EVERY DAY AS A PORTAL TO ACCESS HIGHER LEVELS OF CONSCIOUSNESS. FOR THAT IS WHAT THIS LIFE IS. DON'T WAIT. EVERY BREATH IS AN ASCENSION OPPORTUNITY.

Why would we resist our evolution? Because we all hold a subconscious program that knows,

If I move towards this and truly go where I'm being invited to go, I will lose my comfort zone even more, and surely I'm already at my edge! Why are you asking me to go further? Why are you asking me for more? Life's good. Why would you want me to agitate myself out of this?

The edge is where we want to be living all of the time. Not in the middle of the comfort zone. We want to constantly shift away from that comfort, which paradoxically will become the comfort zone. So, no, we don't end up torturing ourselves for the rest of our days, but instead, we'll find that the growth zone become the flow state. There's something seismic happening here. If you feel confident, comfortable, and familiar with your intuition, there's an excellent chance you're actually in hiding and stagnating. Flow is movement. Flow is change, right? Flow is not stagnation. And so, if we think about the intention, we keep seeking opportunities to get uncomfortable with our intuition because we are growing. We are evolving. That's the entire freaking point of our lives.

Ricci-Jane Adams

WHAT IS A MIRACLE? IT IS OVERCOMING THE BELIEF IN SEPARATION.

The miracle is the shift in perception from separation to oneness. The miracle is ever-present and works its way into our lives if we accept it. It is subtle and quiet and so easily ignored. Cultivate the conditions to allow the miracle frequencies to flourish in your life. Silence. Stillness. Solitude.

DON'T BE AFRAID OF THE EMPTINESS. THE VOID CONTAINS ALL. MAKE YOURSELF A COMFORTABLE SEAT AND BE STILL THERE IN THE VAST OCEAN OF CONSCIOUSNESS.

Ricci–Jane Adams

I VOW THIS DAY TO REMEMBER I AM INFINITE UNLIMITED CONSCIOUSNESS AND TO ACT ACCORDINGLY.

A vow is not an intention or a goal. A vow is an abiding commitment between you and the Infinite. You take a vow in a spiritual context only if you are ready for self-mastery. For a vow is between you and Self. Self as God consciousness. No one else will hold you accountable, not in the end. In the end, all you have is your relationship with Self, and the quality of that relationship will determine the depth of your commitment. Today, are you ready to become masterful of Self?

YOU ARE PURE CONSCIOUSNESS CREATING YOURSELF INTO MATTER.

This is your reminder to create something of your life that is greater than the external evidence suggests is possible.

HERE'S THE TRUTH. IT IS ALL A WONDERFUL, IMPERMANENT DREAM. WHAT MAGIC ARE YOU GOING TO MAKE WITH THIS LIFE?

In the beginning, this truth can cause grief within us. As we unwed ourselves from the illusion, we can experience a state of hopelessness or despair or lack of meaning. The meaning we had made of our lives has nothing to do with truth. Then, piece by piece, we began to establish a new order, awakening to the reality that, yes, it's a dream, but it's a necessary dream. And as a dream, the laws at play differ entirely from what we believed to be true. We have total creative control, for example. What will you create of your life today from that correct perception?

SURRENDERING JUDGEMENT IS A RADICAL ACT, BUT IT IS POSSIBLE. WE BEGIN BY LETTING GO OF THE ADDICTION TO JUDGING OURSELVES, AND NEXT UP, WE STOP JUDGING THE WORLD.

Judgement is the denial of acceptance of what is. It is toxic, and it is also passive. It is rarely followed up by action. Acceptance leads to radical action. I accept this is how it currently is, and I'm willing to act, play my part, and correct the error. At the global and personal level, it remains true. What action will you take to contribute something more significant to the world? What action will you take to contribute to a more incredible version of yourself? This is how we change the world, not through judgement and blame but by taking personal responsibility for our own lives and the global community.

Ricci–Jane Adams

*YOU DIDN'T GO ANYWHERE. YOU NEVER
LEFT GOD. YOU SIMPLY PLACED SOME
OF YOUR CONSCIOUSNESS IN THIS
EARTHLY EXPERIENCE, EARTH SCHOOL,
AS A WAY TO TRAIN THAT
CONSCIOUSNESS TO HOLD A HIGHER
TRUTH, TO HOLD ITSELF IN HIGHER
ESTEEM.*

*BE ALL IN. BE ALL THAT YOU ARE.
DON'T PLAY IN THE ILLUSION. REVEAL
IT FOR WHAT IT IS. THIS IS THE WORK.*

Ricci-Jane Adams

I SEEK ONLY MY ILLIMITABLE EXPANSION BEYOND ALL IDEAS OF MYSELF.

I sat down to journal on a particular fear with this question in my mind - is there something to be genuinely worried about here? The response was swift - *you have no right to be concerned.*

To worry is faithlessness. It is to doubt God. It is to doubt myself. My responsibility is to stay away from the wasteland of worry. My task is not to seek comfort for my littleness but to expand my consciousness into those places of contraction. I can feel the cracks in the false identity growing to let the light in. I'm on the precipice of the next movement of awakening. I humbly welcome letting go of another layer of false control.

LIVE AS THOUGH YOU HAVE NOTHING TO LOSE. BECAUSE YOU DON'T. YOU HAVE NOTHING TO LOSE. WHAT A BLESSED RELIEF.

No matter what we think we want in the dream of this life, nothing will satisfy us except this. Freedom. Not freedom in the dream - holidays, money, power, travel, things - but freedom of our consciousness. Unlimited expansion of consciousness is our birthright and our deepest longing. The conditions in which we attain this are those in which we become less concretised and attached to the dream of this life. Consciousness conveys itself to us through our Intuitive Intelligence. The more time we spend in communion with intuition, perceiving through our spiritual sight, the more free we are.

Ricci–Jane Adams

WE DO NOT CHANGE REALITY AT THE LEVEL OF THE DREAM. IT IS OUR CONSCIOUSNESS WE MUST COMMIT TO MASTERING TO CHANGE THE ILLUSION OF OUR WAKING LIFE.

THE INFINITE INTELLIGENCE OF THIS CONSCIOUSNESS EXPERIMENT WILL ARRANGE EVERYTHING FOR THE MOST RAPID AND EFFICIENT AWAKENING. OUR ONLY TASK IS TO USE WHATEVER CONDITIONS ARE PLACED IN FRONT OF US TO AWAKEN.

It is time to overcome the idea that our spiritual path should make us more comfortable. The spiritual path is the most radical of them all. It is revolutionary. It is the power that creates reality. The perceived 'sickness' we see in the collective reflects how we have used our spirituality like despotic tyrants tending to our ego's wants. The word sovereign is used a lot in the world right now, usually to indicate that the 'right' choice has been made, according to our own sense of right or wrong. There is no right or wrong—sovereign means to possess ultimate power. And we do, as the dreamers of this dream.

Ricci–Jane Adams

I AM A MULTIDIMENSIONAL, COSMIC CONSCIOUSNESS MASQUERADING AS A HUMAN BEING.

FEAR

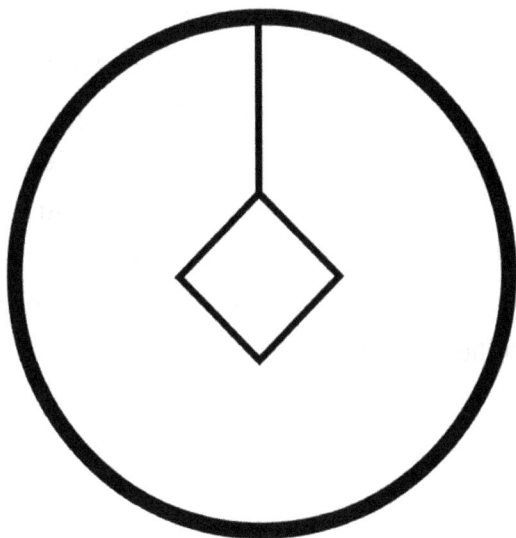

I WILL NOT LET FEAR BE MY COMPANION TODAY. I CHOOSE TO LIVE WITH COURAGE AND GRATITUDE TO BREAK THE HABIT OF FEAR. I CHOOSE TO ALIGN WITH THE HIGHEST PART OF ME.

To be witnessed in our power, connection, and remembrance of Self is a rare and precious wonder. It can move mountains and melt away lifetimes of fear. All fear is one fear. Don't make a bedfellow of fear. Be curious and willing to explore fear, knowing it contains the keys to awakening. And on the other side is power—true, abiding, all-encompassing, grace-infilled power.

WHEN YOU OVER–IDENTIFY WITH YOUR FEAR, YOU FORGET HOW MUCH POWER YOU HAVE. AND THE MOST POWERFUL WAY TO SHIFT OUT OF YOUR FEAR, YOUR WOUNDS, YOUR DOUBT? SACRED SERVICE. YOU ARE MORE FREE TO CHANGE THE WORLD BY ACTS OF SERVICE THAN YOU CAN POSSIBLY KNOW.

Ricci–Jane Adams

I VOW THIS DAY TO MEET MY FEAR.
I AM NOT AIMING FOR FEARLESSNESS.
I AM SIMPLY WILLING TO BE FEARLESS
IN THE FACE OF FEAR.

We evolve through meeting our subconscious fear programs. The aim isn't to avoid fear (which we can also think of as the shadow aspects of ourselves). The objective is to be willing to sit with and meet the discomfort as it rises, to make space for curious and loving investigation. Our fear might have kicked off in response to someone or something outside of us or an inner thought, but the work is always an inside job. In meeting our fear, we meet ourselves. This is evolution.

I'LL JUST BE OVER HERE MEETING MY FEAR, CLEARING MY DOUBT, ENCODING MY REALITY AND ALIGNING WITH MY PURPOSE.

Ricci-Jane Adams

BREAKING FREE OF MY SUBCONSCIOUS FEAR EVERY DAMN DAY IS MY PRAYER TO THE INFINITE SAYING, 'I AM WILLING'.

The actions we take are the demonstration of our faith. Everything we do is a prayer to the Infinite calling in our next life phase. We must ask ourselves if our actions match our faith, and if not, course correct. If they do not align then fear is the reason why. Instead of being motivated by love, our actions are motivated by fear. Go fear hunting to set yourself free.

SPEAKING OUR TRUTH IS NOT ABOUT PROJECTING OUR UNMET FEAR ONTO SOMEONE ELSE. IT IS ABOUT PUTTING DOWN OUR FEAR AND REMEMBERING WHAT WE ARE.

Let's be clear. Speaking YOUR truth is not the same as connecting to THE truth. Your truth right now will change as you evolve. So, just because you've upleveled your consciousness doesn't mean you are there yet. Likewise, don't project your unmet fears and insecurity onto another and claim that as your truth. Surrendering to THE truth is what we're here to do.

THAT FEELING OF AGITATION IS A VERY GOOD SIGN OF YOUR EVOLUTION. TRUST IT.

This path of awakening can sometimes feel challenging. Sometimes, we may wish that we could turn away from the journey. Take courage, dear one. Let the agitation, the holy rage, the restless energy be the fuel that fans your devotional fire. Go deeper into your practices. Dedicate more of your life to the benefit of others. Make service to the greater good your mandate, and you'll find a channel for that evolutionary energy. It is worth it. Stay the course.

MY SPIRITUALITY IS NOT MEASURED BY HOW COMFORTABLE I MAKE YOU FEEL. I WOULD SAY THE OPPOSITE IS TRUE.

My spirituality is not performative. It is not about gaining credit with the world or being approved of, or being thought of as God. My faith is the path of deep work, a fearless intimacy with God. It tends to make me less polite and less tolerable in a domesticated world. I have withdrawn my sense of self from the dream of this life. I am at home with myself in the Infinite. I am sovereign. My love is more profound and more real, but in a world that approves of niceness and false positivity, you might find me unpalatable. I'm ok with that.

Ricci-Jane Adams

YOUR SUCCESS IS INEVITABLE IF YOU LET ME LEAD, DEAR ONE. ARE YOU WILLING? - YOUR HIGHER SELF.

We find this the most challenging task of all. To surrender to infinite intelligence instead of making decisions from the subconscious fear program of our history. It is wise to draw on life experiences. Still, we are responding so often from the basement of subconscious fear rather than lived wisdom (which means we have neutralised the emotional charge of our experiences). Don't make choices from unmet fear. Sit with your fear. Sit with the discomfort. Get to know what is truly motivating you. This is freedom.

FIRST, WE MEET OUR FEAR. THEN, WE CREATE SPACE FOR THE EXPERIENCE OF OUR GOD NATURE.

Fear is the friendly ally directing us home to our God nature. When fear shows up, it allows us to get to know ourselves better. As we do that, we come to the stunning realisation that *I am that.* I am. Know thyself, then, you shall know the universe and God. Fear serves us to do this as the internal GPS signifying that we have lost our bearings on our truth. Follow the fear home.

Ricci–Jane Adams

WHAT IF THERE IS NO PROBLEM?

As a spiritual seeker, I was particularly good at using personal development as a weapon of self-destruction. I could quickly identify all my personal failings and the back story to them with ease. But it brought me no peace. I was always at odds with myself. In that moment of cracking open in response to this question, what was concealed for so long became clear. The perfect version of me didn't exist. The need for it kept me from my own happiness. And the problems of my life, well, were they? No matter how grievous, painful, humiliating, shameful, despairing, or enraging my experiences, they were just life. It was my story about them that made them good or bad. And when I saw it in that way, I was free to live life. I was no longer defeated by it.

WE DO NOT ENGAGE IN A SELF-CENTRIC SPIRITUALITY TO BYPASS OR SILENCE OTHER PEOPLE'S EXPERIENCES. WE LISTEN WITHOUT DEFENSIVENESS, NOT TAKING THINGS PERSONALLY. EVEN WHEN IT IS HARD AND INCONVENIENT, WE WILL DO THE WORK OF DISMANTLING OUR FEAR.

I vow this day. I vow to do the deep work of a deep faith. The shadow. Fear in all its forms. This is what I work with because this is the site of my return to holiness. I am not afraid. I am not afraid for you or me. The fear is the wound and the healing all at once. I seek only the truth. I see with the fearless gaze of compassion. I meet my fear, restore my shadow to light, and dismantle my subconscious programs on behalf of all. This is the only work that matters.

I AM WORTHY BEYOND BELIEF. I AM THE ENTIRE UNIVERSE IN ONE SUBLIME BODY. I BOW TO THE TEMPLE OF MY OWN BEING.

External validation and approval is a drug stronger than any I have met. It gives the highest highs and the lowest lows. It keeps us on a roller coaster of emotional chaos. We can never get enough. We're always needing more to satisfy the emptiness within. There's no power in chasing the temporary high of someone else's opinion. However, we're likely just as addicted to the low of rejection. Either way, we've given ourselves away. And there is no power in that. Come home.

FEAR IS NOT THE PROBLEM. LET IT HAVE ITS WAY WITH YOU. IT IS HERE TO CORRECT THE ERROR.

What's moving in you right now? Fear is the messenger. Listen deeply. Anger is fear. Rage is fear. Injustice is fear. Stress is fear. Anxiety is fear. Hopelessness is fear. Let it alter you. Listen to it. It's guiding you home. Something is wrong. Listen. You're being called back to the truth. But you must sit in the fire of your fear. You must walk through it. There is no going around this. Where am I in denial? Where must I correct the error? Be with the fear. Let it move to you to evolve. Don't bypass it. Don't numb it. Let it be your teacher. This is the shadow work. What have I been holding within me that goes against my truth? Seek it out. Witness it. This is the healing, individually and collectively. It is our divine responsibility.

Ricci-Jane Adams

DECOMPOSE YOURSELF.

Just when you think there's no more to surrender, there is always more. The deep work of a deep faith is the work of surrendering all illusion. And what is illusion? All of it. It's all a glorious and terrible consciousness experiment. Decomposing samsaric longing, letting the layers release, all the shit we've been clinging to - let it become fertile ground for love and truth. But we cannot rush this decomposing phase. Tear down old structures and let yourself cast off what you are not before you claim a new truth. I am not that. I am not this. I am unbecoming. I am dissolving. I am nothing before I become everything. This is a noble and humble phase of awakening that will visit us many times in our lives if we do the deep work. Sometimes we are creating, and sometimes we are destroying. And it's all divine.

OUR MOST SACRED TASK IS TO GO DOWN INTO THAT BASEMENT OF OUR SUBCONSCIOUS AND CLEAR OUT THE UNMET FEAR AND INVESTIGATE IT FOR WHAT IT IS, WHICH IS SIMPLY A COLLECTION OF BELIEFS THAT HAVE PROBABLY HAD THEIR TIME.

Don't let your life be a collection of outdated beliefs that you keep unconsciously recycling reality. Take action today to break the outmoded patterns of behaviour that keep you trapped in your littleness. Today. Today is the divine blessing you are seeking. This breath and this. Step into a new paradigm simply by embodying a new idea of yourself. Get comfortable with being uncomfortable. Align with your mission. It will not land in your consciousness if your life is not congruent.

Ricci-Jane Adams

MEETING FEAR IS ALWAYS A DEATH. IT IS A DEATH TO THE EGO. IT IS THE BEGINNING OF LIFE.

There will always be a period of disorientation as we move away from the known into the unknown. This is what meeting fear is. It is the death of the personality, the little self, to meet who we are beyond our limits. This is the path of the sacred seeker. To be comfortable with the paradox, to sit in that river of change, and to be unafraid. And so we'll often scramble back to the shore that we've known because at least then we don't feel adrift. But to sit in a disoriented state is to be unafraid to meet ourselves as that Infinite consciousness. Disorientation. We will be able to sit in that flow state, sit in that state of grace whilst being disoriented, if we can change our perception of ourselves and no longer feel like victims of our reality.

TO LIVE BEYOND OUR FEAR LIBERATES OUR CREATIVE VISION AND ALLOWS US TO LINE UP WITH WHAT WE ARE TRULY MEANT TO BE EXPRESSING IN THIS LIFE.

Dear God, expand my sacred vision so that I may bear witness to the full expression of your plan for me. Let me be moved beyond my limited perception of myself so that I may inherit the unlimited truth of what I AM.

And so it is.

And it is so.

Ricci–Jane Adams

I RELEASE MY DOUBT, MY FEAR, MY SOCIETAL CONDITIONING THAT TELLS ME I AM NEVER ENOUGH. THIS FAR AND NO FURTHER.

WE MUST STOP AVOIDING OUR FEAR BECAUSE AVOIDANCE OF OUR FEAR IS WHERE WE DEVELOP ADDICTION AND NUMB OURSELVES TO OUR INTUITIVE KNOWING.

Ricci-Jane Adams

*HEALING CAN OFTEN LOOK LIKE
DEATH AND DESTRUCTION. THERE IS
NOTHING TO FEAR IN THIS. CHAOS
BRINGS NEW LIFE. LET IT DIE. LET
THAT OLD ENERGY GO. TRUST THE
PROCESS OF UNBECOMING.*

*I WAS NOT BURIED. I WAS PLANTED.
AND IN THE TIME OF DARKNESS, THE
SOIL HAS GROWN RICH. THE GROUND
OF MY BEING IS IN FULL BLOOM. I AM
ALIVE ONCE MORE.*

Ricci-Jane Adams

INTUITION

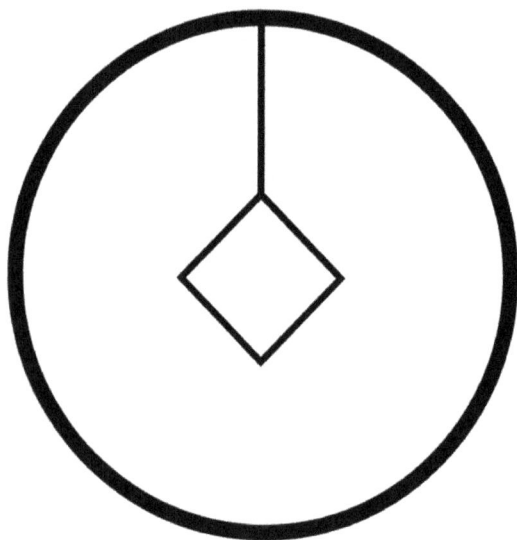

INTUITION IS ABOUT INCREASING OUR SPIRITUAL SELF-ESTEEM. IT IS ABOUT UPREGULATING OUR FREQUENCY. IT IS ABOUT SHOWING UP TO OURSELVES AND GETTING AS UNCOMFORTABLE AS REQUIRED TO BREAK FREE TO THE TRUTH OF OUR SACRED POWER.

Ricci–Jane Adams

*DEEP INTUITION IS FOR THE HUMBLE
IN SERVICE TO THE WORLD. IT IS
UNCOMFORTABLE, ENRAPTURING
EXPANSION. IT WILL ASK YOU TO
FORGET TO REMEMBER. TO LOSE
YOURSELF TO FIND YOUR WAY HOME.*

THE FIRST STEP TO BECOMING WILDLY INTUITIVE IS TO BECOME WILDLY SELF-LOVING. TO BE FULLY UNAFRAID OF OTHER PEOPLE'S OPINIONS OF US SO THAT WE MAY THEN NOT RESPOND FROM A DOMESTICATED, POLITE AND ULTIMATELY NUMB SPACE.

The path to being the most powerful intuitive begins with the willingness to change our minds about ourselves. We must be willing to see ourselves for what we are - one with the God mind, the unified field, the Infinite. Do I know that I am pure, unlimited consciousness? If we are willing to shift our perception of ourselves, we must be willing to do the work of meeting and releasing all the subconscious blocks to our truth. This is how we increase our intuition to the level of Intuitive Intelligence and increase our power to serve.

Why are deep states of intuition harder to maintain? Spiritual self-esteem is required to live in continuous communion with the God mind. If we develop our intuition without increasing our sense of our sacredness, our will always remain shallow. Intuitive Intelligence is the highest and deepest state of intuition. It is intuition as a state of being. We must perceive ourselves as God knows us—infinite, unlimited consciousness.

I BOW BEFORE THE TEMPLE OF MY BEING. I AM ALTERED BY REVERENCE FOR MY FIERCE SPIRIT. MY LIFE IS AN OFFERING TO ONENESS. I FALL AT THE FEET OF THE DEPTHS OF MY INTUITIVE KNOWING. I AM THE ORACLE I SEEK.

Intuition is built on trust. Trusting in something greater than the self, and also trust of the Self, which is One. I am that I am. You must be willing to recognise that your life and its unfolding is connected to something greater than your individual identity.

Ricci-Jane Adams

DEAR GOD, ENCODE ME. IMPRINT ME.
ENGINEER ME IN YOUR IMAGE. I AM
YOURS.

We are never actually seeking the increase of our intuition. We are seeking the development of our consciousness. Increased intuition is the beautiful byproduct of this greater intention. This is how we change the collective experience for all. Why does intuition matter? Because we awaken to the divine heart that resides in the collective consciousness, and we permit, at the deep subconscious level, for all to awaken to this divine heart within. This is the end of separation. This is the end result of intuition.

INTUITIVE INTELLIGENCE IS KNOWING I AM WORTHY OF BEING ONE WITH WHOM THE GOD/DESS SPEAKS.

Spiritual self-esteem unlocks a living, breathing, wild and fierce intuition. This is Intuitive Intelligence. We must be prepared to know that She is speaking and open to receive.

Ricci–Jane Adams

MAKE LOVE TO YOUR FEAR TO MAKE
SPACE FOR YOUR WHOLENESS. REJECT
NOTHING. EMBRACE IT ALL. BRING
ALL PARTS OF YOU HOME.

Intuition is not about getting the Infinite to answer our insecure ego self's mundane and fearful questions. In its full expression, it is surrendering to our unlimited self, merging our consciousness with the One Mind and living in the glowing state of grace. As soon as we contract in fear, we step out of that state and know that we must course correct. That's it. This is our birthright.

INTUITIVE INTELLIGENCE COMES WITH SPIRITUAL MATURITY.

Don't seek out your intuition if you're unprepared to grow spiritually. It is a divine responsibility.

Ricci–Jane Adams

INTUITION IS THE YEARNING FOR CONNECTION TO GOD CONSCIOUSNESS.

Intuition flourishes when we make time and space for stillness, silence and solitude. These are the conditions in which it is easiest to connect to our God consciousness, which constantly communicates with us but so differently from how we communicate through our dominant senses so that we can easily miss it. You are yearning for that communion with Self. Make space for it every day.

FEELING COMFORTABLE ISN'T A SIGN OF YOUR INTUITION.

Don't aim to get comfortable or safe. These are illusions of control. When intuition comes calling with the next steps of your life, it can be as uncomfortable as hell as you recognise all the places where you are incongruous with what God wants for you. What God wants for you is so much bigger than your comfort zone. Feeling comfortable isn't a sign of your intuition. It's simply familiarity. And that familiarity deceives you into thinking this is what you want. It isn't what you want. That sharp feeling of discomfort shaking you out of your comfort zone is your intuition agitating you awake. Rousing you from the slumber of this waking dream that you're pretending is you living your best life. Intuition is like the grain of sand in the oyster. It will reveal itself as the pearl, but you must work for it. You're being called on a grand adventure—the greatest of them all, to journey to the very purpose of your life, which is to meet yourself as God.

Ricci-Jane Adams

INTUITION IS THE BEGINNING OF RECOGNISING FROM WHERE OUR POWER COMES.

The inevitable endpoint of the development of our intuition is a permanent shift in perception. We change our minds about ourselves as we meet our unlimited, infinite consciousness within. We don't just 'tap into' our intuition when we want to answer a question. Instead, we live our intuition, we trust our intuition, and we act upon our intuition without doubt. This is intuition beyond the trinkets and superstitions of the new age. We need nothing outside of ourselves. Because we have changed our minds about what we are, we now understand that we are the oracle, for we are one with the Infinite. This is the end of separation.

*INTUITIVE INTELLIGENCE IS MOVING
BEYOND THE POSSESSION OF
INTUITION TO THE INHABITANCE OF
IT.*

Ricci-Jane Adams

YOU ARE IN POSSESSION OF A FULLY FUNCTIONING, GLORIOUS INTUITION. DO NOT DOUBT IT.

You didn't miss out. You possess a glorious intuition. It's your spiritual superpower. Yet, you do need to work for it. Create the conditions of stillness, silence and solitude every day. If you can't connect to your Intuitive Intelligence, you're not creating the conditions. It's that simple—practice, practice, practice. Then, take action on what you receive. If you keep asking and never act, your intuition gets dull.

YOU KNOW IT'S YOUR INTUITION IF IT SCARES YOU A LITTLE (OR A LOT).

What often makes us believe a choice is 'right' is our comfort level. That's not an indication of intuition. Certainty indicates an intuitive choice, but that doesn't necessarily come with comfort. It can be scary, but we still know it's right! Intuition often feels the strongest and most evident when we have a big choice because the stakes are high. We will quickly know what is right intuitively and make the higher choice. But then comes that ache for the familiar and the known, in other words, the comfort zone. The ego does everything possible to drag you back to the same old life. This is where we've got to dig deep into our spiritual self-esteem and stay away from doubt. The more we trust our intuition, the stronger it gets. Don't be afraid of getting uncomfortable. Intuition is strong when change is coming. Flow with it, and let your life be infused with grace. This is Intuitive Intelligence.

Intuition leads you away from your comfort zone because intuition is part of your soul's evolution process. Your intuition is not a way to get a cosmic guarantee that everything will go according to your agenda. Intuition really gets going when we surrender to divine will. Then we're no longer afraid to *hear, feel, see, know* our intuition. When you have an agenda, you aren't open. You're still thinking like a human. Your intuition is opening you to think like the Universe.

YOUR INTUITION NEVER LED YOU ASTRAY. YOU ARE SIMPLY STILL IN THE PROCESS.

Dear beautiful one, please trust the timing of your life. Trust your joy. It is intuition encoding itself into feeling. Keep going in that direction. But go deeper. Be patient. Keep the faith. The Infinite is conspiring to bring you all that is yours. Get to know yourself. The more you understand about yourself, the more you trust your intuition.

INTUITION WILL ASK THAT YOU FALL IN LOVE WITH YOURSELF.

When we go towards our intuition, we are going in the direction of our power. It is an aphrodisiac as we get closer and closer to the truth of our gloriousness. Our fear has veiled our power and beauty for so long. We didn't know what we were. Intuition awakens us to the truth of what we are, and when we really let it in, we'll be so deeply in love with ourselves that doubt will have no place.

YOUR INTUITION WILL AGITATE YOU AWAKE IF YOU DON'T PAY HEED. DON'T RESIST IT. LET IT LEAD.

A deeper, more lasting, vaster truth calls you to awaken. Intuition leads the way. But please make space for this still, subtle voice to be heard. It cannot reach you through the chaos of the dream you think is life. Take moments to transcend the dream and commune with the Infinite. This is what intuition is.

Ricci-Jane Adams

YOUR INTUITION IS YOUR SPIRITUAL SUPERPOWER. OWN IT.

You've got it by the bucketload. It is you. It's not a gift. It's a fact. Make friends with it. Make it your primary relationship! Intuition is you in communion with yourself, that vaster than the cosmos, infinite intelligence, creator of worlds that you have forgotten yourself to be! Wake up. You are not abandoned on an unfriendly planet with no way to return home. Intuition is the lifeline to your truth. Cultivate a deep and lasting love affair with it now.

Love Notes to the Divine

INTUITION IS A STATE OF BEING.

Beyond the trinkets and superstitions of the new age, intuition is a state of being that we cultivate with devotion and humility. Intuition is communing with God consciousness, and nothing outside of us will activate that conversation. We must be willing to see ourselves as one with the One Mind and then devote ourselves to living from that unified consciousness. It is overcoming the belief in separation. And it is worth every effort. Go within.

Ricci-Jane Adams

YOUR SUCCESS IS INEVITABLE WHEN YOU LIVE FROM YOUR INTUITION.

It's simple. Intuition is the conversation between you and Infinite consciousness. The commitment to your devotion determines the quality of that conversation. When you privilege it above all else, your intuition is a clear, true bell ringing through the darkness and eliminating all doubt. You are listening to the Infinite. You are acting upon the word of the Infinite. Your success is inevitable for you are the hands and feet of the Infinite in the world. And so it is.

JOY IS NOT LIKE HAPPINESS. IT IS DEEP WITHIN, UNCONNECTED TO EXTERNAL REALITY AND THE BRIDGE TO THE DEEPEST INTIMACY WITH THE DIVINE.

Intuition shows up through our feeling states. I'm not talking about clairsentinence here. I'm talking about the often difficult-to-accept truth that our feelings are indicators of our intuition. Why is that difficult? We often want something different from what our intuition is showing us. But no matter how hard we try, we can't ignore that we don't feel connected anymore to what we desperately try to hold onto. It might be a relationship, a career path or a sense of self. So often, our joy is our intuition in disguise, but because we don't know how to make our joy work, we discredit it. Don't do that anymore. Trust your joy. Go in that direction even when it is hard. The Infinite is calling you. You won't get the next step on the path until you take the first.

Ricci-Jane Adams

INTUITION ISN'T REALLY A CONVERSATION AT ALL. IT IS OVERCOMING SEPARATION TO MERGE WITH THE GOD MIND TO LIVE FROM INSIDE THAT TRUTH.

Intuition is not something outside of us that we pause to ask questions of. It's not something we ever need to question at all. Intuition is, when trained and practised with devotion, a state of being. What does that mean? It means we're in a flow state of knowing right action in each moment, consciously sometimes, but most importantly, subconsciously. We don't have to stop and ask because we have switched our subconscious belief pattern from no trust to trust. We are in flow with the highest order. God is guiding us.

Love Notes to the Divine

YOUR SUCCESS IS INEVITABLE WHEN YOU LIVE FROM YOUR INTUITION.

Intuition is our spiritual superpower. Our task is not to look for the best psychic or tarot card reader. Our mission is to train our innate intuition because we ALL possess it. We all have access to the God Mind, and there all knowledge resides. We can prepare ourselves to have laser-like access to this Infinite field. This is our birthright, and it is how we optimise our lives.

Ricci–Jane Adams

INTUITIVE INTELLIGENCE IS THE PATH TO OVERCOMING THE BELIEF IN SEPARATION. IT IS THE PATH TO LOVE.

EVERY INTUITIVE HIT, EVERY BIT OF INSPIRATION IS A PRECIOUS OFFER THAT GOD IS LAYING BEFORE OUR FEET. A PRECIOUS JEWEL SAYING, 'I AM GIVING YOU THIS PIECE OF ME, I WANT YOU TO TAKE IT FORWARD AND CREATE IN MY NAME'. AND HOW OFTEN DO WE KICK AWAY THOSE MOMENTS OF INSPIRATION AND SAY, 'NO, I'M NOT GOOD ENOUGH?

Ricci-Jane Adams

THE DEVELOPMENT OF OUR INTUITION IS A REFLECTION OF THE DEVELOPMENT OF OUR CONSCIOUSNESS. INTUITION IS A SPIRITUAL FACULTY, NOT A NEW AGE TRINKET.

Your spiritual seeking is a privilege, and there will be days when it feels like a hefty burden, but I want you to remind yourself not to be afraid of the discomfort. Don't be afraid of getting uncomfortable. That's evolution. It's evidence of change, and that's an excellent thing. It's okay if not every day is sunshine and roses. Eventually, that time will come, but we must work for it. Not to earn it, not because someone's keeping a scorecard up in heaven, but because it is the law that we must be congruent between our beliefs and our actions in the world, and until we are, we're breaking the law.

THE ESSENTIAL AND OFTEN MISSED PHASE IN THE PROCESS OF AWAKENING IS THE COMMITMENT TO LIVE IN A WAY THAT SUPPORTS THE INCREASE OF YOUR INNATE INTUITION TO THE LEVEL OF INTUITIVE INTELLIGENCE. HOW DO WE DO IT?

- Stillness, silence, solitude daily
- Eat lightly and consciously
- Walk or sit in nature if you can, even if it is simply gazing at your favourite indoor plant
- Move your body
- Meet your subconscious fear with conscious intent
- Do at least one thing in holy service
- Read a sacred text
- Bathe if that's available to you
- Start and end your day intentionally
- Find pleasure in the mundane chores by becoming fully present as you do them
- Introduce digital sundown at least two hours before bed

- Limit anything that alters your state of consciousness
- Laugh
- Express appreciation.
- Alter your vibration at will by cultivating a feeling state disproportionate to evidence

Every conscious breath is an opportunity to develop intimacy with the divine.

I ACHE TO BE MET IN THE DEEPEST THROES OF INTIMACY WITH MY INTUITION. I LONG TO BE MET AS I AM, CONCEALING NOTHING, AND WITH EVERY BREATH MOVING CLOSER TO GOD.

Ricci-Jane Adams

I AM NOT AFRAID OF MY LIFE AND ALL THE MESSY, GLORIOUS TRUTH THAT COMES WITH IT.

I am not afraid to flow where my Intuitive Intelligence takes me, even if I do not yet know what it will bring. I am so open to life. So willing to be present to it. It is the sublime song of the language of consciousness - intuition - always leading me, that makes it possible to heal without struggle, to perceive with grace. To live in flow with superconsciousness is bliss. But it is not easy. It comes with the willingness to sweat for God. To do the deep work of a deep faith. This is what is demanded to become superconscious.

IT HAS TAKEN ME DECADES TO HAVE THE COURAGE TO FOLLOW MY INTUITION TO ITS FURTHEST REACHES, BEYOND WHAT IS COMFORTABLE AND ACCEPTABLE TO MOST OF THE WORLD. TO BECOME CONGRUENT WITH WHO I HAVE ALWAYS SENSED MYSELF TO BE. BUT HERE, NOW, I AM.

Ricci-Jane Adams

*BE NOT AFRAID OF YOUR INTUITION.
BE UNCONCERNED WITH FOLLOWING
IT WHERE IT LEADS. SIMPLY PREPARE
YOURSELF AS THE HOLY VEHICLE
THAT YOU ARE SO IT CAN FIND A
HOME WITHIN YOU. LET YOURSELF BE
A RESTING PLACE FOR YOUR
INTUITION TO LAND.*

How do we prepare ourselves to be a resting place for our intuition to land? It takes intention, devotion and commitment. Intuition does not arrive into an unprepared vessel.

MYSTICISM

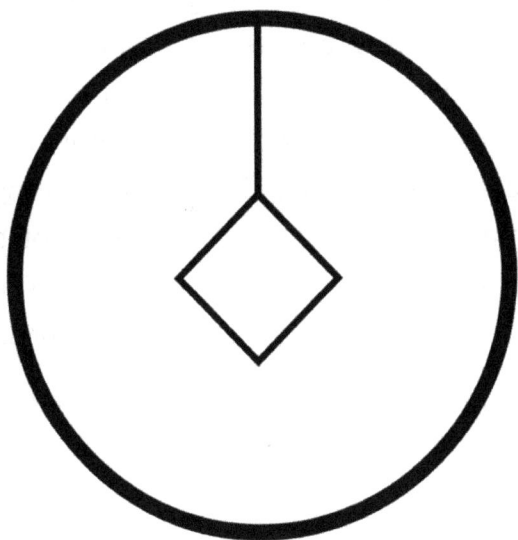

Ricci-Jane Adams

SHE'S GOT THAT WHOLE PRIESTESS, MYSTIC, LEADER OF A NEW PARADIGM VIBE.

These are my kind of women. They are not superficial, jumping from one shiny distraction to the next. They are not seeking more knowledge to hoard it. They desire to serve through it. They are doing the deep work of a deep faith to embody ancient wisdom. They know they are here in this life to serve the greater good. They are anchoring a new paradigm. They are self-sovereigning, not seeking the world to recognise or approve them. They seek only to be right with God/dess consciousness.

YOU ARE BEYOND EVERYTHING YOU BELIEVE ABOUT YOURSELF. YOU ARE VAST AND ANCIENT. YOU ARE FIERCE AS FUCK. I BOW TO YOU, SISTER. NOW GO MAKE THIS LIFE HAPPEN WITH YOUR TRUTH.

We are all elevated in the presence of women who are really doing the work. It's a palpable energy that takes up space, alters matter and benefits all. In the presence of women who are congruent between heart and mind, faith and actions, we are all blessed with the possibility of embodying a deep spirituality.

Ricci-Jane Adams

PLEASE DO NOT DOUBT HOW DEEP AND ANCIENT YOUR SOUL IS, DEAR SISTER. YOU HAVE SERVED THE AWAKENING OF ALL FOR LIFETIMES.

In case you're having doubts today, please don't. You've walked this path for lifetimes. You are born to do it, and yes, many others have incarnated at the same time for the express purpose of serving the collective awakening. So when you look around and see so many other women doing similar work, take courage that you're not doing this alone; they are not your competition, and where we are going, we can only get to together. I bow to the women doing the deep work. Keep going. You are glorious.

I AM THE MYSTIC. I AM ALIGNED WITH THE DEEP MYSTERIES OF THE COSMOS AND UNAFRAID TO BE A MYSTERY TO THE WORLD.

You don't need to explain your mystic self to a mundane world. Be self-approving. If you need the world to confirm your right to be the mystic, then you've missed the point. The mystic's primary relationship is with God. Go there to meet yourself, into that divine reunion with Self. What is outside you in the dream will never quench your mystic's deep thirst to know herself as God/dess. Become self-reliant, which is to say God-reliant.

Ricci-Jane Adams

THE MYSTIC KNOWS TO BECOME NOTHING TO BECOME EVERYTHING.

Why are we so afraid of the void? It is here we attain access to our infinite nature. Beyond words, beyond ideas, beyond the dream, that's where we go to meet ourselves. We return renewed, electric with possibility. Let the beliefs melt away today, dear one. You're so much more than you've yet imagined. This is what the mystic in you knows. Listen to her and let her lead the way.

Never be afraid of giving up belief and all your ideas of yourself. Who you are exists beyond belief. The less you believe about yourself, the closer you are to your God nature. All these definitions are dead weights that prevent you from awakening to truth. You are God consciousness, pure and unlimited. Any other category, definition, diagnosis, quiz, map, or chart fixes you to time and space. You are anchored into a false, temporary reality that gives the ego satisfaction and even relief from the personal responsibility of coming home to the truth that you are God. Read that again. Despite our yearning to come home, we desperately yearn to be relieved from the divine responsibility. Don't fall for it. Become nothing. It's the only way to meet yourself as what you are.

Ricci-Jane Adams

THE MYSTIC IS SPIRITUALLY FIERCE. HER WORK IS IN THE WORLD, BRIDGING HEAVEN AND EARTH.

The mystic is the demonstration of her faith. The work she does in her devotion is for the world's benefit. She is the bridge between form and formlessness. The vibration she holds is her service. She holds the possibility for a new paradigm. She is the transpersonal guide—the bridge between the mundane and the divine.

THE MYSTIC IS THE SYMBOL OF HOLY POWER.

We are so afraid of power because when we survey the world, what screams back at us is how power, especially supposed holy power, has been abused and used. But the new paradigm belongs to the Priestess energy, and she is grounded in humility and grace. She is power because service is her mandate, measure, and meaning.

Ricci–Jane Adams

*THE MYSTICAL WOMAN IS THE
ULTIMATE WILD WOMAN. HER
PRIMARY RELATIONSHIP IS NOT WITH
THE WORLD. YOU CAN NOT EVEN
TOUCH HER MAGIC.*

To all my mystic sisters, stay true to you today. And every day. The world may not get you, but I do. I see your soul yearning to meet you at deeper and deeper levels, the vastness of your calling, and your holy desire for Union. Keep going. Keep privileging this relationship. Let it be your guide. You are birthing a new paradigm for all.

MY PRIMARY RELATIONSHIP IS WITH GOD/DESS.

My primary relationship is with what is real and eternal. This is how I lay down my arms and end the war within. This is what it is to be a mystic—to privilege this truth. In the world we inhabit, very little allows us to honour our mysticism. Make space within you for her as an offer to the world.

I FALL IN LOVE WITH ANY WOMAN WHO SHOWS ME HER INNER MYSTIC. THERE'S NO MAGIC THAT COMPARES TO THE MYSTICAL WILD WOMAN.

A woman who has emancipated herself from the world's illusions is free. She has met herself at the deepest levels of her being, which is to say she has met herself as God/dess. She fulfils her own soul's desires. She goes within to claim her power. She is 100% self-approving.

The mystic woman is in the world but not of it. She has withdrawn her truth to a higher power, which conversely makes her more available to the dream of this life. Because she now knows who and what she truly is, she's no longer afraid to love with Fierce devotion and create a life of her most extraordinary imaginative reckoning. She knows too much to hold back. She explores her soul through the illusion of the world.

MYSTICISM IS A PATH INWARDS TO MEET OURSELVES AS GOD/DESS. NO THINKING OR LOGIC OR DEMANDING CAN GET US THERE. WE ACCESS OUR INNER MYSTIC'S DEEP AND ANCIENT POWER THROUGH STILLNESS, SILENCE, SOLITUDE, PRAYER AND SELF-REFLECTION.

The dream of this life is very distracting. It will make us believe that our faith is a luxury or only useful when trying to get something or make something happen. Don't judge yourself for this phase. It is necessary. And then the shift occurs. We begin to surrender because the pull is irresistible, and everything else becomes a distraction. We yearn to be with our God/dess nature in every moment. Not to leave the world behind but to bring our devotion to it. Our devotion becomes an act of service to a weary world. We make an offering of our faith. It is an active faith that we demonstrate in our lives, our relationships, our work. We are doing the deep work of a deep faith. This is what it is to privilege the interior life. The mystic's power is an unstoppable force for grace to enter the world.

WE ARE NOT A PUZZLE TO BE SOLVED. WE CANNOT KNOW OURSELVES THROUGH REASON AND DEDUCTION. WE CAN ONLY MEET OURSELVES BEYOND THE ILLUSION OF THE RATIONAL WORLD. I'LL MEET YOU THERE IN THE STILLNESS, SILENCE AND SOLITUDE OF MY BEING.

A mystic's work is to become fully conscious. They do not do this by analysis but rather by sitting in the mystery of their existence. In making peace with the mystery and paradox of their being and making space for that truth, they become fully aware and awake. Solving the mystery doesn't get us any closer to our truth.

I AM IN LOVE BEYOND ALL REASON WITH HER. I PRAY DAILY THAT, FOR HER, LIFE IS AN UNLIMITED BOUNTY OF WONDER.

Who are you? Are you loyal to her? Do you show up for her? Sweat for her? It's so easy to lose the truth of ourselves to the demands and noise of the world. Stay present to your truth. Perhaps it's a truth you are only just becoming conscious of. Especially as you begin to awaken to your sacred power, it is vital that you are fiercely loyal to this emergent truth of your being. And we are constantly emerging to ever more profound levels of truth no matter how long we've been on this path.

Ricci–Jane Adams

WE'RE THE WILD MYSTICAL WOMAN. WE'VE BEEN CALLED EVERY NAME. WE ARE BEYOND ALL YOUR IDEAS OF US.

The Mystic's Manifesto.

We no longer hide our light, give away our power, and make others comfortable. We live on the margins, in the shadows, beyond the known. We're unreasonable because the mystical inspires us, and the nonlocal guides us. We're not wedded to the dream. We're dangerous because you cannot touch our magic. We don't belong to the man-made world but are willing to enter it to dream a better one for all. We're fierce as fuck and outside of all expectations. We're quicksilver, as Pandora tells us. We're idealised, adored from afar, placed on altars, but rarely encountered up close. Because if you let us near, we'll drag you to the underworld of your being and hang you on the hook of your liberation. We're fear huntresses, truth seekers, and change makers. We're the wild, mystical woman.

THE MYSTIC IS THE FULLY EMBODIED EXPERIENCE OF THE DIVINE. THERE IS NOTHING COMPROMISING ABOUT HER. SHE IS HOLY FIRE, BURNING AWAY ILLUSION.

You exist in divine perfection. Beyond the clutches of the little ego self, you are always the highest expression of your infinite truth. Access to her is possible at every moment. The choice must be made to stay loyal to your awakening before anything else. The choice must be made to do the deep work of a deep faith to live a congruent life. The choice must be made to adore your precious life and make bold leaps in faith.

Ricci-Jane Adams

FAITH

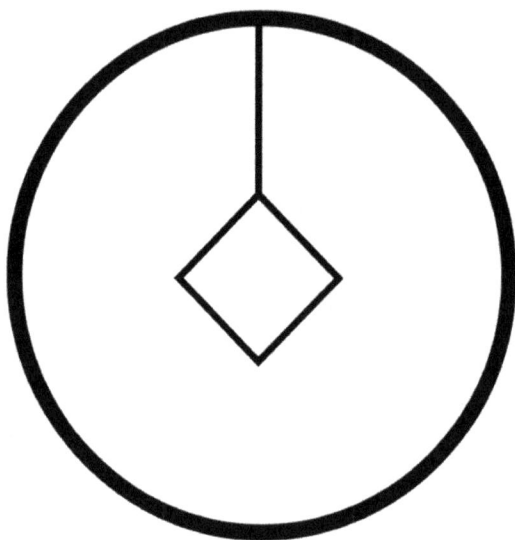

DESTROY YOUR REPUTATION AT EVERY OPPORTUNITY. KEEP YOURSELF ON YOUR TOES. BE BORN ANEW. LET GO OF YOUR IDEAS OF YOURSELF AND HUMBLY BOW BEFORE THE GODDESS, ASKING THAT YOU INITIATE YOURSELF BEYOND THE WORLD OF IDEAS AND IDENTITIES. UNLEARN YOURSELF.

Ricci-Jane Adams

FAITH IS ACTIVE. DO THE WORK.

Please don't tell me that nothing changes if you are doing nothing to change. Faith is active. You've got to show up to your devotion to create a new paradigm, personally and globally. Be fierce in your devotion, and don't take the easy route, looking for something outside of you to alleviate the intensity of meeting yourself as unlimited consciousness. It will not always going to be easy, simple, or comfortable. There's nothing wrong with getting uncomfortable. It's the beginning of freedom for us all.

YOU ARE THE FREAKING LOVE OF YOUR LIFE. BE CRAZY LOYAL TO THAT LOVE, AND EVERY OTHER RELATIONSHIP WILL WORK.

The quality of your relationship with yourself determines the quality of your relationship with the world. What you offer yourself is precisely what you offer others and God. Your life is your service. Your relationship with yourself is the only relationship that needs to improve in order to improve every other relationship you have, including the one with the Infinite. You must see yourself for what you indeed are, which is infinite and unlimited consciousness.

NO MATTER WHAT ELSE HAPPENS TODAY, I WILL HOLD ONTO THE TRUTH THAT I AM A HOLY, FIERCE, POWERFUL WARRIOR GODDESS.

This is your reminder that you have everything you need to rock this life. You've got magic they haven't even seen yet. When you remember who you are beyond the ego ideas of Self, you connect to the ancient, vast truth of your being. Hang out there and bring it into manifestation in the world. Rely on your real power source.

WHEN YOUR FAITH AND ACTIONS MATCH, THE EXTERNAL REALITY ALIGNS WITH WHAT YOU FEEL IN YOUR HEART FOR YOUR LIFE.

Even if the details of your best life are unclear, the feeling is probably palpable. So, go away from the mundane and the ordinary and towards that feeling. If the vision is clear, then protect it! Don't agree to anything less than that vision. God has assigned you a mission. Honour it.

Ricci–Jane Adams

*STARTING THE DAY WITH THE
PURPOSE OF GETTING CLEAR AND
INTENTIONAL CHANGES EVERYTHING.
THE INFINITE ADORES ACTION–
TAKERS!*

When we act on our faith and invest in our beliefs, we demonstrate our willingness to go further on the journey of our lives. It is the space in which intuition comes alive because we are clearing the vessel to allow more God consciousness to pour into us.

STAY. IN. YOUR. OWN. LANE. DON'T LOOK OUTSIDE OF YOURSELF. BE FIERCE IN THE PURSUIT OF WHAT YOU ARE CREATING.

You are the creator of your vision. Protect it, even if others don't understand or doubt you. Be fiercely loyal to you and your creation. I see you. I honour you. You're doing so good.

LET THIS BE YOUR MANTRA TODAY – I ADORE CHANGE.

If you can feel the truth of this in your bones, even if it scares you, then you are one of the sacred leaders of our age. Most of us battle and rage against change as though IT is the problem. It is our resistance to change that causes our suffering. And change, for those of us who lead the new paradigm, is the only and greatest evidence of growth. Evolution does not happen in a static environment. Chaos births higher order. Be with what is with radical acceptance, surrendering to higher truth and unafraid to let go of old ideas. Willingly. Release. Your. Agenda. Let God lead. Change is inevitable, necessary, constant and glorious. It leads us ever closer to truth. Bow down to it. And witness your evolution unfold with greater power.

GO WHERE YOUR AGITATION LEADS YOU INSTEAD OF BURYING YOURSELF ALIVE IN THE KNOWN.

What would it take for you to follow your soul's lead and abandon your comfort zone? Not because you know what will happen but because you don't know, and that's the point. Stepping into the unknown is the only way to evolve. I am not asking you to create emotional chaos where there isn't any. I am asking you to stop ignoring the signs when they appear. Follow the lead of your soul. Let God lead. The growing pains are your evolution, even when it feels scary.

Ricci-Jane Adams

*DO THE DEEP WORK OF A DEEP FAITH.
THIS IS FROM WHERE THE POWER OF
YOUR BEING EMERGES.*

Please, dear one, do not press the set and forget button on your inner life. It's from whence we create our reality. Everything begins and ends with the world within the world. Your inner being is your Higher Self. It is your God nature. It is the creative authority. Don't be so distracted by the exterior dramas and plays that you abandon your inner life. It will not feel good, and nothing will satisfy. Go within. Let this be from where you build your vision.

WHAT IS A MIRACLE? IT IS YOU CHANGING YOUR MIND ABOUT YOURSELF.

A miracle is a shift in perception from human sight to God sight. We are upgrading our vision to perceive ourselves as God sees us. When we are willing to change our minds about ourselves and give up our littleness, we are freed to become our truth. Our truth is our service. If we're not shining, we're in darkness. Our service is our medicine. What we give to ourselves, we offer to all.

Ricci-Jane Adams

IT'S YOUR TASK TO SEEK FOR THE TRUTH OF YOURSELF AND THEN LIVE IN CONGRUENCE WITH THAT.

What is acting in integrity versus people pleasing? To privilege your own life doesn't mean being selfish or narcissistic. It means *know thyself.* Spend time investing in unpacking all the programs to discover who you are. And then be totally loyal to yourself. You are your own medicine. When you water yourself down to keep others happy or stay in situations that don't serve you, then you're betraying yourself. And that hurts. It delays your evolution. It's not your job to keep everyone happy.

BEGIN WITH THE CHOICE TO FOLLOW THAT HIGHER PART OF YOURSELF, EVEN IF YOU HAVE NO FREAKING IDEA WHERE IT IS GOING TO TAKE YOU.

Whatever it is, don't wait another moment to become the full expression of what you are. You cannot fail when you choose for love. Knowing the difference between your love choices and fear choices might take some time because fear choices often look like acts of great love. They're acts of not trusting, self-doubt, seeking external validation, fear of change, martyrdom, fear of rejection, perceived loss of power, and the list goes on. Get clear with yourself by spending time in the stillness of devotion. The loving choice is often the more challenging choice. But honouring oneself is the only way to honour another.

Ricci-Jane Adams

PRESENCE IS THE ANTIDOTE TO EVERYTHING THAT AILS ME. IF I AM HERE, I AM HOME.

Presence means allowing each moment to guide us to the best course of action. When we allow ourselves to be present, we tune in to what we feel bodily, emotionally, and energetically. In a quantum understanding of the universe, all is one. All time and space is one. If we are obsessed with past events, living our history, not letting go of things, unforgiving, holding on to our pain, then we are not home. We are not present. Likewise, if we're constantly terrified of the future, we're never available in the present. When we're in fear of what has happened to us in the past or what might happen to us in the future, we aren't present.

We must be willing to cultivate presence as part of our commitment to increasing our access to our Intuitive Intelligence.

*KEEP ON TRUSTING. KEEP ON
SURRENDERING. KEEP ON PUTTING
DOWN YOUR AGENDA. KEEP ON
WAITING ON GOD'S INSTRUCTIONS.
THIS IS FAITH. YOU'LL NEVER FAIL.*

Ricci-Jane Adams

SACRED SERVICE & DEVOTION

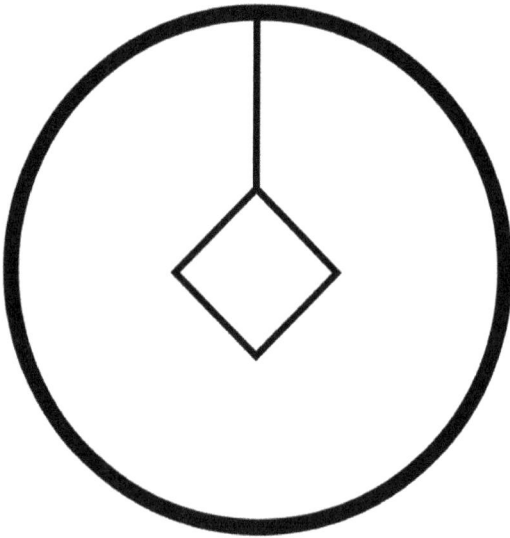

DEAR GOD,
INCREASE MY POWER TO SERVE.
AND SO IT IS.
AND IT IS SO

Ricci-Jane Adams

OUR SPIRITUAL AWAKENING IS IN SERVICE TO OUR ALL-NESS NOT TO OUR EGO IDENTITY. WE WANT TO LIBERATE ALL BECAUSE WE REALISE THAT IS WHAT WE ARE.

It is not about you. The juiciest paradox of all is that we must become nothing to become everything. We often turn up to our spiritual path seeking to become 'something'. Or to get something. Or to fix something. We are motivated by the desire to improve ourselves, make more of ourselves, to awaken ourselves. Very quickly, we come to understand that it isn't about us at all if we are doing the deep work of a deep faith. In surrendering the idea of us as an individual consciousness, we truly begin to awaken.

OUR SPIRITUALITY IS ABOUT SACRED SERVICE, AND WE MUST BE UNAFRAID TO LEAD.

Ricci–Jane Adams

WE WORK TO PUT DOWN OUR LITTLENESS TO MEET OUR LIMITS TO INCREASE OUR POWER TO SERVE. IN SO DOING, WE CAN GUIDE OTHERS TO THEIR HOLY POWER.

PLEASE GO BIGGER WITH YOUR VISION. IT'S TIME TO THINK LIKE THE UNIVERSE.

This is a call to action. Put down your littleness and take up more room. Get louder. Let yourself feel the bigness of your vision. Let it thrill you and terrify you. If it feels comfortable, then you're probably on autopilot. I'm not talking about money or clients or any of that. I'm inviting us all to feel that we have no limits. When we feel into the vastness of the Cosmos, we recognise that we are feeling into our truth. Expand into the unlimited consciousness you are. Do it every day. I'm not referencing the number of people you serve or the amount of money you make when I ask you to go bigger with your vision. Instead, I'm asking you to consider how willing you are to be free, how happy, how unafraid you are to meet your fear, how wide open are your arms to embrace everything with love. When you know what you truly are, your vision is unlimited.

Ricci-Jane Adams

TO CREATE THAT VISION YOU HOLD IN YOUR HEART, IT IS OK TO SAY NO TO THE ORDINARY.

At some point, it's inevitable that you'll be called to make a choice. You'll be asked to end your relationship with the ordinary to go where your soul is calling you. This might seem like an easy decision, but like many mundane marriages, the comfort is its own kind of aphrodisiac. You can't take the comfort zone with you. So prepare for that day, that day of days, by resisting the illusion of the comfort zone and staying alive to the possibility of your life in every moment. Make way for the gloriousness of what God wants to bring into the world through you.

THERE IS A REASON WHY YOU ARE HERE AND A READINESS WITHIN YOU TO ACHIEVE YOUR PURPOSE.

You have everything you need to fulfil that deep call inside of your being. You were born ready. We don't activate our purpose because we keep saying no to our intuitive knowing. We say no because we recognise that things will have to change. And some of us prefer to die unrealised than sit in the discomfort of change. Don't be that person.

Ricci-Jane Adams

BE THE DEMONSTRATION OF THE BEING ON FIRE WITH PURPOSE SO THAT OTHERS ARE SET FREE JUST BY YOU BEING IN THE WORLD.

Purposeful energy is magnetic and contagious. You inspire the very atmosphere around you! You are a blessing to everyone because you lead by example. The oak seed is optimised to become the oak tree. Its full magnificence is housed in that tiny seed. And so it goes with us. Most people live way beneath what is possible for them because they have no evidence that more is possible. Be the evidence that human consciousness is waiting for.

WE DON'T TURN UP TO THIS SPIRITUAL LIFE BY ACCIDENT. IT SEEKS US OUT MORE POWERFULLY THAN ANY OTHER IMPULSE.

Our only path is to remember ourselves as God consciousness. Infinite and unlimited. It is the only purpose. We all share it. There are a billion-plus ways to walk the path and, we will all do it. Surrender. Give yourself over. It is the call of an irresistible lover. Give in to the most tremendous impulse you've ever felt. Let it lead you home. Nothing else matters, and all will work itself out when you do.

Ricci–Jane Adams

IT IS IN THE STATE OF MEDITATION THAT WE CREATE OUR LIVES.

Take a moment or an hour to reflect on the quality of your devotion. Where can you go deeper? What stories have you been telling yourself about why your devotion, meditation, prayer, journaling, and chanting can wait until you're less busy? Here's the thing. Life will continue to happen. There will never be the quiet day you're hoping for unless you choose it. And the sooner you centre your devotion, the sooner you'll see the life you want to be living appear in reality. In the stillness, silence and solitude, we meet with our infinite nature and encode consciousness. We can cultivate a deep faith and do the deep work. It takes a willingness to change up our routines and overcome our habits. We can lose ourselves so easily in the noise of life. Make a home for your soul daily.

WHEN IT COMES TO DEVOTION WHAT MATTERS IS WHAT WE DO WHEN NO ONE IS WATCHING.

Our devotion can be measured by what we do when no one is watching. Performative spirituality is the opposite of this. It's what we do when we have or are trying to gain an audience for ourselves or, get pats on the back, or any kind of need to be witnessed on our path. Will you stay the course of your awakening even if no one ever knows your name or asks about your journey? Do the deep work of a deep faith. Our spiritual awakening will positively impact everyone, but not because we posted about it. Because there is only One consciousness, and when we do the deep work, we do it on behalf of all.

Ricci-Jane Adams

AS WE RECLAIM OUR GOD SELF, WE CONTRIBUTE TO THE AWAKENING OF ALL SENTIENT BEINGS. WE NEVER AWAKEN FOR OURSELVES ALONE. IN TRUTH, THERE IS ONLY ONE OF US HERE.

There is only One. I am. I am that. I am that I am. This is how we live our faith. There's only one of us here. Are my actions a match for that truth?

NO LONGER CAN WE SIT IN INACTION AND SPIRITUAL APATHY. WE ARE BEING INVITED TO MEET THE TIMES IN WHICH WE LIVE WITH THE WILLINGNESS TO CHANGE AND AWAKEN ON BEHALF OF ALL.

Spiritual awakening is not an optional extra, a hobby, or a brand. It is the only purpose of our lives. Everything in the dream of this life serves that purpose. Our task is to utilise the events of our time to evolve our consciousness on behalf of all. We are experiencing a spiritual zeitgeist. But how many of us are offering our spiritual path in service to the collective awakening? If you are in hiding in any way about your spiritual path for fear of judgement, then you cannot be fully available to the world. Step out of the closet. It isn't about preaching to unready ears. It is about being congruent between your faith and your actions. Show up. Meet your subconscious, ancient wounds about persecution and show up. The world is waiting for the spiritual revolutionaries to emerge.

FROM THE MILKY OCEAN OF CONSCIOUSNESS I AM BORN, AND IN THAT FIELD OF PURE POTENTIAL I RETURN TO RENEW MY WEARY SOUL.

Rest your soul today. You may not be able to stop entirely or change your plans or the demands on your time but, give your soul what it craves (stillness, silence and solitude) for even five minutes, and everything will improve. Resting your soul is not the same as resting your body, although you'll often experience fatigue in your body because your soul's needs are not being met. You are soul first, body second. Bring full consciousness to everything you do today, and it becomes devotion. Your soul will be happy.

BE UNREASONABLE IN THE PURSUIT OF YOUR PASSION AND PURPOSE.

This is the key to a well-lived life. A full and deep devotion to your very existence. A willingness to go fearlessly in the direction of something great within you. This is the path of the Priestess Mystic Leader for the truth is, this is how we serve. A half-lived life serves no one. It's OK if the details of your purpose are unclear. Know this. The details will come. Our purpose is the same as everyone else's—to be here in service by commitment to our awakening of consciousness.

Ricci-Jane Adams

YOU ARE THE REASON YOU ARE HERE IN THIS LIFE, AND YOU ARE THE ONLY ONE WHO CAN FULFIL THE DEEP LONGING OF YOUR BEING. BE YOUR OWN BELOVED.

THIS IS YOUR PERMISSION TO PRIVILEGE YOUR RELATIONSHIP WITH YOUR SOUL ABOVE YOUR RELATIONSHIP WITH THE WORLD.

Nothing in the world around us makes it easy to be the mystic. But if the mystic is part of you, and she is never given space, stillness and solitude, you'll likely be in a state of torment. What you're craving is within. It takes time to unlearn the addiction to the world of the superficial senses, but it is time worth taking. Every time you show up to your mat or your cushion, it gets easier. You are attuned to your highest intelligence and most glorious truth. Devotion is the key. Make it daily, if not more.

Ricci-Jane Adams

MY SOUL IS MY FIRST PRIORITY, NOT MY LAST. THE GROUND INTO WHICH I AM ROOTED. THE TEMPLE OF MY CREATION. THE MEETING PLACE OF THE HOLY AND THE MUNDANE. THE REASON FOR MY BEING. THE ONLY TRUTH. THE BEGINNING AND THE END AND THE EVERYTHING IN BETWEEN.

There is no life without my soul. There is no purpose more significant than the remembrance of that truth. Except perhaps to serve from that place. To put my spirituality into a radical form of service is the highest aim. When we live from this place, all else finds its highest ground.

Love Notes to the Divine

EMBODYING THE SACRED IS THE SHIFT FROM, WHAT MAY I GET BY SHOWING UP TO MY SPIRITUAL AWAKENING? TO WHAT MAY I GIVE? HOW MAY I SERVE?

137

Ricci–Jane Adams

THE MORE YOU PUT DOWN YOUR NEED FOR YOUR EGO'S DESIRES TO BE MET AND INSTEAD SAY, 'HOW MAY I BE OF SERVICE TO THIS ONENESS THAT IS ME?' THE MORE YOU DO THIS YOUR LIFE WILL BECOME SO FREAKING BLISSFUL YOU'LL WONDER WHY YOU DIDN'T DO IT SOONER.

AWAKENING IS RECOGNISING THE CAGE. DEVOTION IS THE PATH TO GETTING OUT OF IT.

Ricci-Jane Adams

I'M NOT HERE FOR THE LIKES. I AM HERE IN PURSUIT OF MY TRUTH. MY SERVICE IS MY MEDICINE. I CANNOT GUIDE YOU IN A WAY THAT IS LESSER THAN I GUIDE MYSELF.

Take personal responsibility for the world that you see. When you deny your intuition and decline your wild and beautiful soul, you contribute that inferior offer to the world. I do not share this to shame you. Instead, to inspire you. You have the power. You are the medicine. Live boldly, wildly free, pursuing the expansion of your consciousness as liberation for all. Let's not waste any more time perpetuating the suffering nightmare. Be the demonstration

TO BETTER UNDERSTAND THE NATURE OF REALITY, GLOBAL EVENTS, THE BIGGEST EMOTIONS, AND YOUR PLACE IN THE WORLD, BE HUMBLE ENOUGH TO TAKE IT INTO YOUR HEART, TO THE MAT, TO THE TEMPLE, ON THE KITCHEN FLOOR, WHEREVER YOU FIND YOURSELF. AND WITH AN ATTITUDE OF DEVOTION, ASK ONLY THAT ALL BLOCKS TO LOVE ARE REMOVED FROM YOUR HEART.

In the stillness, silence and solitude, through repetition and commitment, day by day, moment by moment, the illusion falls away. Sometimes all at once and sometimes painstakingly slowly, until the blind faith is almost run out, and then all at once, the light breaks through into the darkness. Surrender comes then, tears too, body slumping in relief as the tightness and restless longing abates. Surrender into the infinite embrace of the Cosmos. Devotion leads us home to truth. Don't look in the dream for the answer. Seek only the soul.

Ricci–Jane Adams

GRACE & JOY

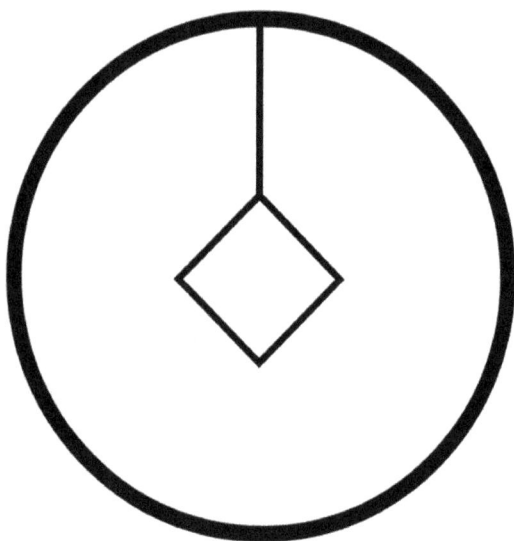

CONTROL IS THE OPPOSITE OF GRACE. GRACE EXISTS IN SURRENDER TO HIGHER POWER.

When everything feels out of our control, go with grace. In a limitless Cosmos, choice is the act of creation. The divine paradox here is that I may not get to say when, how, or in what way my outer reality shows up, but I am always choosing my response to it. Eventually, it's inevitable that the two, inner and outer, will become one because this is the law of correspondence. But at first, it is the act of surrendering the ego's false sense of control to surrender to a higher power - that is what grace feels like. Surrender to the highest part of ourselves, having wrestled back authority for our lives from the ego-identified self.

Ricci–Jane Adams

I LIVE BY GRACE. I AM RELEASED BY GRACE. I GIVE BY GRACE. I RELEASE BY GRACE.

GRACE IS WHAT WE ARE. IT IS A STATE OF BEING THAT IS FREEDOM FROM FEAR.

Grace is part of the path to sacred leadership. We can only lead from this place once we experience ourselves as the divine. Privileging our inner mystic is the fastest way to see our power increase in the world. We think it is the other way around. Grace is experiencing ourselves as a God consciousness. What could be more remarkable and more important than that? Make it your daily goal.

Ricci-Jane Adams

*MOVING IN THE DIRECTION OF OUR
JOY IS ABOUT BECOMING A
VIBRATIONAL MATCH FOR THE
HIGHEST PURPOSE OF OUR LIVES.*

We think joy means something along the lines of getting our ego's insecurities met, superficial happiness and human ideals of success. That's not what we are talking about here at all. It might be the more challenging path. It will certainly require discipline, and undoubtedly, things will change. People will judge you, and you'll wonder if you have what it takes. Keep going, dear one. Your joy is not temporary or fleeting. It is awakening. It is union. It is where we are all destined to go, this lifetime or the next.

YOUR LIFE IS YOUR GREATEST CREATIVE FREEDOM.

Collectively, we have set a low bar on what we consider a well-lived life. All of us are leaders in waiting. What we lead is the creative authority of our own lives. This requires getting really connected to who we are and what we desire. We then must have the courage to make choices that are congruent with that truth. This is where we falter, and we accept so much less, someone else's idea, for example. We live someone else's life and wonder why we are always unsatisfied. Your life is your greatest creative freedom. What are you doing with it? How are you living? Is it your truth? Or is it supporting you to discover that truth? Don't waste one more moment waiting in the vestibule of your life. Open the door and walk through.

Ricci-Jane Adams

THERE IS NO TOP OF THE MOUNTAIN.

The key to sacred power is to be humble enough to remember this and to get down on our knees before our God nature and offer ourselves to that grace. That is when we remember our only power is God's. This path of awakening is not linear. Life events are not a measure of your spiritual evolution. Your response to them is.

THE MIRACLE CAN ONLY BE RECEIVED BY US AT THE LEVEL WE ARE READY TO RECEIVE IT.

We receive the miracle or the answer to the prayer at the level that we are ready to receive it. What determines that readiness? We are prepared to receive only if we are unafraid. If the miracle is too big for our level of consciousness for where we're currently sitting, then we will reject it. We do this all of the time. We reject the benevolence of the universe. We reject the miracle because our fear triggers us. What happens when we raise our vibration and open to our intuition is that fear comes up. In some ways, the miracle has been too big for where our consciousness is sitting. I say, Who wants that? I want to be ready for all of the miracles, all of the time. How do I do that? I change my vibration at will and regardless of external evidence.

Ricci–Jane Adams

*I WANT NOTHING BUT WHAT I HAVE
AT THIS MOMENT.*

*I HONOUR EVERYONE AS THEY ARE
TODAY.*

*I SEEK NOT TO CHANGE OR BE
CHANGED.*

*I ACCEPT THE BLESSING OF THIS
BREATH.*

*I OVERFLOW WITH APPRECIATION FOR
PRESENCE.*

HERE I AM.

AND SO IT IS.

OH MY DARLING, IF ONLY YOU COULD SEE THE INNOCENCE I SEE. THE WORLD HAS NOT TOUCHED YOU. YOUR ACTIONS HAVE NOT DIMINISHED YOU. YOUR PERFECTION REMAINS INTACT IN THE EYES OF THE UNIVERSE.

You are so worthy. The Universe will never stop holding you close and whispering to you the purpose of your life. Lean into this warm embrace. You are unforgiven, for you were never judged. Your intuition is evidence of your union with the divine. And it is always there waiting for you.

Ricci-Jane Adams

EVERYTHING IS UNFOLDING AS IT SHOULD EVEN WHEN I DO NOT UNDERSTAND. IT IS THE ARROGANCE OF THE EGO THAT LEADS US TO SEEK THE FALSE CONTROL OF KNOWING WITH THE MIND. TRUE UNDERSTANDING NEEDS NO EXPLANATION.

YOU CANNOT FAIL, MY DARLING, WHEN YOU KEEP MOVING IN THE DIRECTION OF YOUR JOY.

I put myself first. What does that mean? It means I keep moving fearlessly toward my joy, even if it means disappointing others. To put myself first is the opposite of selfish. It is self-sovereignty; it is how I create a paradigm shift so that others may be set free and put themselves first. A joy revolution!

Ricci-Jane Adams

SPIRITUAL FIERCENESS

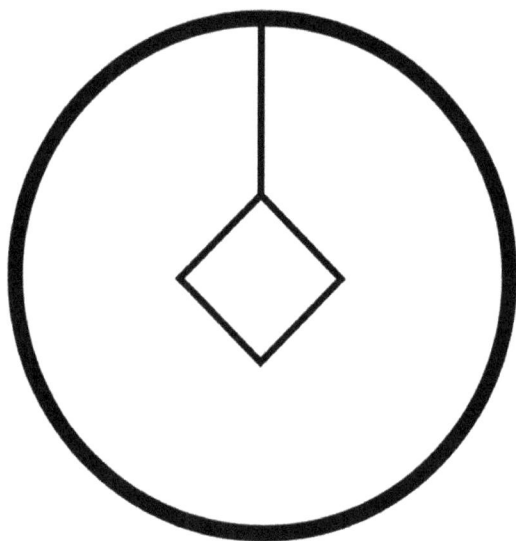

WE MUST GIVE UP UNWORTHINESS NOW AS AN ACT OF SERVICE TO THE PLANET.

At some point on this path, we must surrender our ego-identified fear voice that keeps beating us up for our failures. Why must this happen? Because the spiritual path is the path home to our God consciousness. If every step of this path isn't moving us closer to radical self-love, which is to say to have the veils ripped from our eyes and to see Truth then we are not walking yet. Truth is I AM. There is no self-doubt in that statement. The biggest impediment to deep states of intuition is low self-esteem.

Ricci–Jane Adams

IF YOU ARE IN HIDING ABOUT BEING SPIRITUAL, IN YOUR SPIRITUAL CLOSET, THEN WHAT CHANCE DO YOU HAVE TO BRING LIGHT TO THE DARKEST AND MOST UNJUST PARTS OF THE WORLD?

Come out of hiding. Your spirituality is the greatest power there is to change the world. If your spirituality is just 'in private,' then you are breaking the cosmic laws. We are one consciousness, and we evolve together. You cannot awaken in private. Your devotion is your service to the world; if you stay in that closet, then, you're not a spiritual seeker. You're just making yourself feel nice. Own what you are. It's time to action your faith. This lifetime is yours to serve the collective good. You are safe to do so. Put down your past life wounds. We've all died for this work a thousand times. Let's move on. I am here in service to something greater than myself to support the permanent shift from fear to love for all. I'm calling you out, dear one. Come out of hiding and do the work.

*I AM NOT AFRAID OF THE DARKNESS.
I HAVE LIVED FOR ETERNITY.
EMBODIED THE SHADOWS. AWOKEN
TO THE LIGHT. AGAIN AND AGAIN.
I HAVE LIVED IT ALL.*

This is your truth. There will be days filled with light and days consumed by the shadows, but all is One. When we can see that our life is a continuum of experience, we stop judging the individual emotions on individual days. You are ancient, and you have lived it all. This is our truth. Zoom out on your life situation and perception of your problems, and you will remember yourself as God/dess consciousness. Your life events are all serving you. All of them. Serving you to awaken to the truth of what you are. Don't be afraid today. You have lived it all.

Ricci-Jane Adams

HERE ARE THE KEYS TO A FULLY EXPRESSED LIFE: SELF-RELIANCE, SELF-SOVEREIGNTY, SELF-APPROVAL.

It takes deep spiritual self-esteem to enact these things, but my darling, invest in them above all else. Go fiercely in the direction of your freedom. Pursue your sovereignty and let nothing stand between you and your self-determination. You are glorious.

YES YES YES YES YES YES YES.

To all those places you are saying 'no' to yourself out of fear and doubt, please start saying yes. To all the decisions you've let someone else make for you, reclaim yourself now. When they said, no darling, it's not reasonable, you can't do that, it's not worthwhile, you took on their no as your own. Reclaim your wild, embodied, holy hell yes! To all the times you shut yourself down before someone else could. To all the times you have denied the wild and blessed callings of your soul and instead clung to the shores of your comfort zone. The measure of your life's worth is not how secure you are—risk uncertainty. Risk the unknown. Say yes yes yes yes yes to yourself! Say yes to your mystic, your wild self, especially when no one else understands. Are you willing to say yes to your life?

Ricci–Jane Adams

EVERYTHING IS POSSIBLE WHEN WE ARE SELF–APPROVING. DO THE WORK TO FALL IN LOVE WITH YOURSELF.

Self-approval. This phrase has so much more power to me than self-love, mainly because we are so powerfully motivated by external approval that we are set free when we heal that need. Then it's all up from there to total self-love. They are the same thing. You can't be self-approving without loving yourself. But they are phases of the journey, and before we can deeply fall in love, we need to approve of ourselves, back ourselves and detach from external opinions. It's not a one-time decision. It's a commitment to continually ask yourself for your opinion, and then be fiercely loyal to yourself.

I AM UNAFRAID TO LOVE MYSELF SO DEEPLY THAT I RECOGNISE THE DEEP TRUTH THAT I NEED NO ONE OUTSIDE OF ME EVEN TO KNOW MY NAME.

The work is all about withdrawing our sense of self from an imaginary world. It is within that we meet ourselves as God consciousness, and it can only ever be in that relationship that we establish our worth. How much of your day is built around gaining approval or attention or love from the world around you? It's exhausting and leads to an emotional rollercoaster of a life. Check your motives for what you create, what you do, what you say, and what you share. Does it come from a deep sense of connection to Self? If not, you are probably looking to get something from the dream of this life. And it won't bring you what you need. Go within.

Ricci-Jane Adams

TODAY, I WILL NOT SQUANDER ONE PRECIOUS BREATH ON WORRYING ABOUT SOMEONE ELSE'S OPINION OF MY INCREDIBLE LIFE.

Sovereignty. We say we want it. But what if someone disapproves of you? What if you have to say no to someone who expects you to say yes? What if you'll have to take personal responsibility for your life? It takes courage to take the throne of our own lives. We have to learn how to trust ourselves. How do we do that? We turn the volume way up on our own intuitive knowing. Sovereignty and intuition go hand in hand.

I CAN BE BOTH NOT NICE AND DEEPLY SPIRITUAL. SPIRITUAL AWAKENING IS NOT ABOUT BEING 'LOVE AND LIGHT'. IT IS ABOUT CLEARING OUT WHAT IS NOT REAL AND TAKING THE REQUIRED ACTION.

Please stop being a 'good' girl. I'm not talking about goodness. We are indoctrinated into this archetype out of believing that we still need to keep ourselves safe. If you are a grown woman reading this, then you don't have to be good to be safe. To be spiritual. To be loved. Be real, sister. Be fierce. Be soft. Be raw. Be vast. Just do the deep work of a deep faith. Then, your primary relationship is with the Self.

YOUR LIFE IS YOUR PURPOSE.

You are not in this life to be approved of or even loved by another. You are here to learn how to give those things to yourself so you can genuinely provide them to another. Otherwise, all your relationships are codependent. Gifting yourself freedom from the prison of seeking other people's approval is how you grant it to others. It won't be easy, especially if you're a people pleaser, but your life is worth it.

PLEASE, BECOME SELF-APPROVING, SO MUCH SO THAT YOU KNOW YOU DON'T HAVE TO ACCEPT THE ORDINARY AND TRUST THAT THE INFINITE WITHIN YOU WILL PROVIDE.

Letting people down—this has to be one of the biggest fears we have. Why? Because we are terrified of being disapproved of. We have so externalised our sense of worth that we can only measure it by other's opinions of us. Our lives pass us by because we do not have the courage to create the lives our souls yearn to create. We stay ordinary and safe to avoid anyone ever judging us. We prioritise the mundane to prevent ourselves from ever leaping into the unknown. That fear of being judged is fear of failing. What if I try and I can't do it? In trying, you meet yourself and fall in love with her. Please, become self-approving, so much so that you know you don't have to accept the ordinary and trust that the Infinite within you WILL PROVIDE. You have to take the first step before God can meet you.

Ricci–Jane Adams

EVERY CHOICE WE MAKE IS AN EVALUATION OF OURSELVES.

We think self-love means going to yoga or eating right. At its deepest level, it means to privilege ourselves above all else because we remember that there is only One consciousness. If you limit, deny or delay your joy, you are doing that on behalf of everyone. We are the entire cosmos. We are everyone we know. Putting yourself second, third or even last is what you are giving to others. Self-sacrifice is not a loving choice. This does not mean we get to behave badly. Instead, every choice we make is an evaluation of ourselves. Self-approval is the key to a fully lived life. Please don't delay for one more moment the full expression of what you are for one more moment. To be truly self-approving, we need to know our true power source: infinite consciousness.

YOU HAVE FULL PERMISSION TO CHANGE. NOTHING IN THIS SEASONAL, CYCLICAL LIFE IS MEANT TO STAY THE SAME.

Comfort is not an indication of spiritual evolution, and it should not be our highest purpose. Take a quick audit of your prayers, affirmations and goals. You'll be shocked to notice how many of them are veiled attempts to stay comfortable or to get more comfortable. Change, not comfort, indicates your evolution, and that's what we seek on this path.

Ricci–Jane Adams

NO ONE SAID THIS PATH OF AWAKENING WOULD BE EASY. IT DOESN'T NEED TO BE. IT'S OK TO SWEAT FOR GOD.

No one said it would be easy. No one said it would be this hard. This is the spiritual journey. We turn up with a certain amount of awareness that this is a higher path and, like all higher paths, might take a little more sweat. But there is a time that every spiritual seeker will experience, often more than once. The dark night. The loss of faith. The yearning to go back to the start and choose the other pill. To stay asleep in the dream is so much easier on the surface. But the dream doesn't exist, so it is a temporary fix. We will all be agitated awake eventually. It is the single purpose of our lives. So what are you going to do? Ultimately, the doubt will cease, and the continual joy, not temporary happiness, but deep soul joy that the external world cannot shake, will settle into your bones. It's worth it. It's the only way. Don't be afraid of the sweat.

ONE OF THE GREATEST CHALLENGES WE FACE IS TO BECOME SELF-RELIANT. WE LOOK OUTSIDE OF OURSELVES RATHER THAN GOING WITHIN FOR THE WISDOM THAT WE SEEK.

Ultimately, we look outside of ourselves because it is the easier path. We don't have to do the deep work of keeping our holy vehicle, this body and mind, prepared to open to truth. It is entirely true that everything you need is within you. You are the Infinite made manifest. But the vessel must be prepared, and we do that through devotion, discipline, discerning choices and preparing ourselves to listen. It is much easier to seek outside, get the quick fix and hope for the best. The path of awakening cannot be done for you by anybody else, and it is not meant to be effortless. Your effort is your prayer. Be the demonstration of your faith. This is where the miracle enters the situation of your life.

Ricci-Jane Adams

A SELF-APPROVING PERSON IS A DEEP SIGH OF SWEET RELIEF FOR THE WORLD.

Externalising our worth—we do it all the damn time. Don't believe it? Review your actions today and invite in the question, *did I change my innate response to elicit a particular response from that person?* Little white lies to downright self-delusion. We constantly manipulate others to get the approval we can't give ourselves. A self-approving person has a different energy. You know they don't want or need anything from you when they enter the room. They won't edit what they say or do to adapt to the room. They are who they are wherever they go. It's a profound relief to be in their presence, and it's a profound relief to meet ourselves in that way. Withdraw your need for approval from the world.

AM I GOOD WITH GOD?

Subconsciously, even our spiritual awakening may be motivated by the need for approval to gain followers, audience, attention, or fame. In the age of celebrity, we often mistake fame for a successful life. Be vigilant regarding this. Sit in your devotion to meet your true motivation for awakening. You will never know the names of the most enlightened beings on Earth. That is not their function. They operate in the subtle realms. Their bliss is Union. Their needs are few. They do not chase a crowd to witness their journey. Become a witness to yourself. Seek only to be witnessed by your God Self.

Ricci–Jane Adams

MY SPIRITUALITY IS NOT A LUXURY.

This path is not for the faint of heart. Yet, it is the only path, and we will all come to it eventually. When we recognise this truth, we can surrender our resistance and boldly step out and into the work of our lives, which is to awaken. Spiritual awakening is not something we do when life is behaving, we've got enough sleep, our relationships are working and so on. It is not a luxury. When treated such, you'll never find the human balance you seek. Don't be afraid of the wild, untamable call of your soul. When you follow it and build your life from it, then that which you are seeking at the human level of your being will appear. When we make our devotion to service, this happens exponentially.

I AM THAT I AM.

At some point on this path, we must surrender our ego-identified fear voice that keeps beating us up for our failures. Why must this happen? Because the spiritual path is the path home to our God-consciousness. If every step of this path isn't moving us closer to radical self-love, which is to say to have the veils ripped from our eyes and to see Truth, then we are not walking yet. Truth is, I AM. There is no self-doubt in that statement.

Ricci-Jane Adams

WE GILDED OUR CAGES WITH GOLD AND THOUGHT THAT WE HAD BOUGHT OUR FREEDOM.

Gilding our cages is a metaphor for what we've been doing with our spiritual tools. We've been using our spiritual tools to get our ego's needs met rather than for awakening. We're in prisons of our own making. We've painted our cages with all the luxuries that we could possibly manufacture through the law of attraction and using all of these tools to get our ego's needs met, to get a bigger house, larger TV, more stuff, a partner, and a sense of security in a dream, which is just a paradox in itself. And now we're looking around and realising that we are all still in the cages no matter how pretty we made them. It's time to understand what freedom truly is. Freedom has never been about how many holidays we get in a year or how many spiritual objects we buy. These are the avoidances that we have substituted for our soul's longing. Surrender intuition is asking us now to recognise that those things would never meet our needs. It is time to set ourselves free from the nightmare of separation. There is only one of us here.

IT IS OUR JOB TO CHOOSE WHERE OUR BELIEF IS LEADING US. THE MORE WE TRAIN OURSELVES TO BECOME SPIRITUALLY FIERCE, WE WILL STOP GOING ALONG WITH EVERY NEGATIVE SELF-BELIEF WE HAVE.

Ricci-Jane Adams

SPIRITUAL SELF-ESTEEM IS
BREAKING THE HABIT OF BELIEVING
THAT YOU ARE HUMAN ALONE.

THE LIFE YOU LIVE TODAY IS THE LIFE YOU LIVE.

Choice is our creative power. What we choose to include or exclude from our lives is our creative authority. For those of us in the awakening path, is our creative choice aligning our sight with the highest vision? Are we living in accordance with our God nature? The life you live today is the life you live. Today. Make today the day that you make a bold choice that supports you to live in accordance with your bliss? What is that choice for you?

Ricci-Jane Adams

I WANT YOU TO KNOW IT'S MEANT TO BE MESSY, THIS EXPERIENCE OF BEING ALIVE. IT'S WILD, IT'S AN OUTRAGEOUS PROPOSITION. SO RUN TOWARDS IT WITH ARMS WIDE OPEN. HOLD NOTHING BACK.

IF YOU WANT THE HIGHEST VERSION OF YOUR LIFE, THEN BRING THE HIGHEST VERSION OF YOU TO LIFE.

That will be different every day. But whatever you can bring, you must. Don't let any perceived external situation be the reason you sink into meanness, blame, anger, gossip, unkindness, assumption, and small-mindedness. The more you lower the tone, the vibration, of your reality with these actions, the more you will try to find someone else to hold responsible. Be self-governing. Speak if you need to speak. But before you do, look within, take personal responsibility and ask yourself, *Is this true? This story of woe I am telling myself, is this true?* Or is it just a convenient way not to show up in your true gloriousness to life? People become addicted to seeing the worst in others and life events. It is an addiction, but the addiction will obscure that truth from you, and you will tell yourself that life continually lets you down.

Be self-reliant. Be self-sovereign.

Bring the better version of you to your life.

Ricci–Jane Adams

GOD

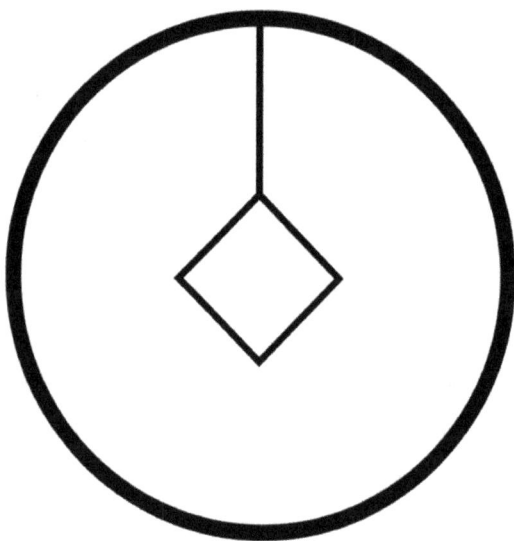

EXCUSE ME WHILE I MAKE EVERYTHING SACRED AGAIN.

I teach people to know that they are God. I do this because my spirituality was superficial for too long, built on trinkets and superstitions. I felt like there was something deeper that I couldn't access, which made me angry with God. My faith was easily diminished when things didn't go my way. I was not rooted in my faith. Yet my soul was relentless in its yearning, pulling me closer to a more profound truth. The truth of how the Cosmos works and how redundant all my fist shaking at the sky had been. God wasn't in the heavens.

God is within me. This is such a big truth that most people turn away or believe it only on the good days when things are 'high vibing' or seeming to go their way. To know that God is what we are takes great courage. How can we do this? How can we be deeply rooted in our truth so that we never move into doubt?

Ricci–Jane Adams

We have to understand how consciousness works, and we have to become masterful in the language of the Cosmos - intuition. It's not always comfortable or easy work. But it is the only thing our soul will settle for. To meet ourselves as the infinite. This wisdom is ancient. It is neither easy nor hard to understand, and it is full of sacred paradox. It can be consumed by the mind but it must be felt by the heart to be turned into the roadmap for our soul. Some days I remember I am God more than others. But I always have the wisdom to bring me home.

IF YOU COULD SEE YOURSELF AS THE INFINITE SEES YOU, YOU WOULD FALL ON YOUR KNEES IN AWE.

Trust yourself. Not your domesticated, tamed, in chains, afraid of your God nature. Your true nature lives beneath your fear. You have to be willing to find her beneath all the layers of shit that have piled upon your glory. Who are you? You are the most incredible adventure of your own life. Go meet her.

Ricci–Jane Adams

THE GRATITUDE IS 100% MUTUAL – GOD.

If you think the Infinite isn't as devoted to you as you are to it, think again. God consciousness is what we are striving for. But God consciousness knows that you already are it! Every time you pray, you bow your head in gratitude, and you express your divinity in the world, the Infinite smiles deeply and makes its own gratitude list about you. We are that which we seek. And it's all Oneness. You are as precious as what you believe you are seeking. I am that I am. And no matter what you do, feel, think or say, the Infinite is madly deeply in love with you.

GIVE UP ALL THE HEAVINESS. KEEP GIVING IT UP AND UP AND UP AND UP.

Oh, dear one. Please stop trying to resolve the situation of your life on your own. Whatever is burdening you, hand it over to God. Hand it over to the Infinite. We hold on so tightly to the things that scare us. What about surrendering it all and saying, *thy will be done*. Let it all go.

Ricci-Jane Adams

I AM NOT AFRAID OF THE WORD GOD BECAUSE I AM NOT AFRAID OF MY OWN POWER. IN THE WORD GOD, I RECOGNISE MY OWN NAME.

YOU HAVE NOT MET YOURSELF IN THE FULLNESS OF YOUR TRUTH. BUT YOU WILL. AND THAT WILL MAKE ALL OTHER DAYS MAKE SENSE.

We are on an eternal adventure to know ourselves. For when we do, we will meet ourselves as God/dess. The journey is not yet done until we live in that infinite, unlimited place. And what a glorious adventure it is! To peel back the layers and move closer and closer to God consciousness. To become intimate with the divine! What a life.

Ricci-Jane Adams

LEAD YOURSELF OUT OF THE DARKNESS. SEE YOURSELF AS YOU WANT OTHERS TO SEE YOU.

It always comes back to a shift in perception. Are you willing to see yourself as God/dess sees you. Not small and limited but infinite and glorious, residing someplace other than this dream and simply projecting an image back into the illusion to awaken to yourself at deeper and deeper levels. What are you conjuring from the dream? Is it heaven or hell? Are you seeing yourself through the veil of illusion or are you thinking like the Universe, and projecting her image into reality?

GOD/DESS ADORES YOU SO MUCH THAT IT CHANGES TO MATCH YOU.

What are you going to do with that truth today? What are you willing to let go of to make the space for what you really want? Reality is simply a match to you. Let go of what you no longer want to increase. Call in your truth. You are a consciousness encoder.

Ricci-Jane Adams

WE HAVE BUILT WALLS BETWEEN OURSELVES AND GOD, AND THEN WONDER WHY WE LOST THE DEEPER MEANING OF OUR LIVES.

What is God? God is what we are. It is the superconsciousness that is us beyond all our fear and doubt. It is all. It is One. We are not separate from God. It is a shorthand for infinite, unlimited consciousness. Our intuition brings us into intimate contact with us, the highest, most sacred and powerful part of ourselves. When we ignore our intuition, we ignore our God consciousness, and we cause ourselves stress, anxiety, depression and disconnection. We have forgotten we are gods. We have forgotten we are God. Turning on and expanding into our intuition connects us to the truth. Intuition is the language of Oneness.

GOD/DESS CONSCIOUSNESS IS WHAT WE ARE. IT IS INNOCENCE. GOD IS HUMILITY, GRACE AND POWER.

Don't let the man-made terrors about God fool you or deny you the blessed intimacy of the divine embrace. The word has power in it. It is a profound relief to reclaim it and to embody the truth I AM that. I am. It's a bold move to rewrite our relationship with God, and it's spiritually radical to determine our own relationship with this infinite power that we are. Once, we were naive, so we rejected God like a teenager rejects a parent who won't let them have their way. Now we are innocent, so we remember we are God, innocence itself.

Ricci–Jane Adams

WE ARE NOT REQUIRED TO SUFFER FOR OUR AWAKENING.

Life will bring events into our lives that will require us to make big, hard, and uncomfortable decisions. When self-approving, we know that we can make these decisions from a place of deep love. The spiritual path doesn't prevent life from happening, but our commitment to awakening means we can face life with a different perception. The perception is, *this life is happening in accordance with my highest good, and I trust it. I don't need to know why things are unfolding as they are. I trust.* The trust is for ourselves in the fullness of what we are, which is God consciousness. Don't be afraid today of the big decisions. Meet them with your higher power. This is your truth.

Love Notes to the Divine

THE HOLIEST WORK IS IN BRINGING INTIMACY WITH THE DIVINE TO THE MUNDANE OF OUR LIVES.

It is so easy to forget our true nature. Our opportunity is to privilege meeting ourselves as limitless. This can be as simple as inviting God into every situation. We tend to keep our mundane chores to ourselves. But what if today you let God lead? In everything? What if today God is in the dishes, in meditation, in ferrying children from one task to the next, in work, and in the pleasure? God is our unlimited self. We can bring that to everything. This is how the miracle enters.

Ricci–Jane Adams

WHO THE HELL ARE YOU TO BELIEVE THAT YOU ARE GOD? WHO THE HELL ARE YOU NOT TO?

Who are we to say no to God when she is calling us? Calling us in. Calling us out. Calling us through that deep knowing in our being that is beyond fear. What is it that you are being called to serve at this time that is being blocked by fear, doubt, self loathing, history, collective emotional contagion, playing small? Now ask yourself, what's on the other side of that? That's the place where she stands, holding the space for your arrival.

BEYOND THE FACULTY OF REASON, A HIGHER FORM OF INTELLIGENCE EMANATES FROM WITHIN THE MULTIDIMENSIONAL HEART.

Intuitive Intelligence is the highest form of intelligence, and when passion and purpose are calling you, it is from this intelligence you are being guided. The multidimensional heart connects you to the One mind. The One Mind guides your purpose. Beyond reason, meet yourself as God.

Ricci-Jane Adams

JUST SAY TO GOD, 'SHOW ME TRUTH. SHOW IT TO ME AGAIN AND AGAIN'.

The path of deep intuition, of Intuitive Intelligence, is uncompromising because it will ask you to put down all perceived limitations and to go directly towards that truth that you are God and that you, too, pre-exist consciousness. What does it mean to say that? It means that you are that which created consciousness. Consciousness is a function of our awakening. It is a tool you use to manufacture a reality that wakes you up to the truth that you are God. Intuition is consciousness in communication. When you remember what you are, you have no more need for intuition as you have understood it for so long. This truly is a revolution in consciousness because what is being asked is not that you simply change your mind about yourself but that you change your mind about the very fabric of existence.

WHEN I SPEAK OF GOD, I AM NOT SPEAKING OF SOMEONE ON A THRONE IN THE SKY KEEPING SCORE ABOUT WHETHER YOU'VE BEEN GOOD OR BAD. GOD IS NOT SANTA CLAUS. IT'S YOU RECOGNISING THAT YOU ARE THAT. YOU ARE GOD.

Are you ready for that? Most of us aren't, so we make God something else or somewhere else so that we never have to meet our holy human power–but it is our only task with this life. To change our minds about ourselves and to meet ourselves as what we truly are. That is why intuition matters so damn much. It is the language of our God-consciousness. It is the hotline to the one mind. But it's not 'out there'. It's in here within you. Embodying intuition and anchoring it into our human beingness is the only way to get truly intimate with our intuition and our God nature.

Ricci-Jane Adams

*GOD IS THE YEARNING IN OUR SOULS
TO UNITE WITH WHAT WE TRULY ARE,
OUR RESTLESS LONGING TO BECOME
WHOLE.*

WHEN WE REMEMBER THAT WE ARE GOD, WE'RE HUMBLE ENOUGH TO NOT MANIFEST FROM A SMALL PLACE. WE'RE TRYING INSTEAD TO SIMPLY, GLORIOUSLY, LIVE IN ACCORDANCE WITH WHAT WE ARE, WHICH IS GOD.

Ricci-Jane Adams

INSTEAD OF TRYING TO MAKE THE DREAM OF THIS LIFE BEHAVE ITSELF, WHAT IF I SIMPLY ZOOM OUT AND REMEMBER MY INFINITE GOD NATURE, WHICH IS THE GENERATOR OF THE COSMOS?

WE ARE GOD'S HANDS AND FEET IN THE WORLD. WE TAKE OUR INSTRUCTIONS DIRECTLY FROM THE SOURCE, EVEN WHEN IT IS INCONVENIENT AND UNCOMFORTABLE.

Ricci-Jane Adams

MY LIFE BECOMES MORE BLISSFUL EACH DAY AS I ALIGN WITH MY TRUTH. THIS IS SOMETIMES IN THE BIG THINGS BUT MORE OFTEN IN THE SMALL, INTIMATE DETAILS OF HOW I SPEND MY TIME. MY OUTER WORLD BECOMES INCREASINGLY A REFLECTION OF MY INNER BEING.

This is how the war stops. This is when the anxiety ends. There is so much pleasure in this intimacy with our authentic truth. It is worth all the sweat to find this for ourselves. Our authentic selves are in there, yet buried so often beneath the rubble of fear, expectations, and external pressure. Most of us have never met this part of ourselves in fullness.What does it take to get there? To be so fiercely loyal to ourselves that we unearth this most profound and beautiful expression of who we are? It is an inner pilgrimage. It is a journey of unfolding consciousness. It is not the work of the gross material plane. Our authenticity lies within, and our Intuitive Intelligence guides us to the inner world of our truth.

I AM THE VESSEL FOR WHAT GOD WANTS. I CANNOT BE LESS OF WHO I AM FOR THAT IS TO SAY NOT GOD. I DO NOT SAY NOT TO GOD.

Ricci–Jane Adams

WHAT IS A WELL LIVED LIFE? TO MAKE CHOICES IN EVERY MOMENT THAT TAKE ME CLOSER TO THE TRUTH THAT I AM GOD. THROUGH JOY, PLEASURE, MOONLIGHT, HEARTACHE, DOING THE DISHES, RAISING CHILDREN, EATING, DANCING, SINGING, SIGHING, GRIEVING. BY BEING FULLY ALIVE TO WHAT IS.

HUMILITY

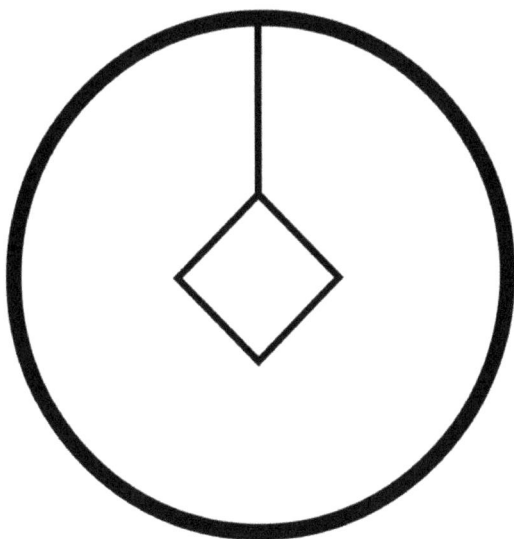

EVERY DAMN DAY WE MUST BE
WILLING TO MEET OUR FEAR.
THIS IS HUMILITY.

Humility isn't playing small. Humility is having the courage to meet our darkest fears, hunt down our shadows, correct the error in our perception and emerge into our gloriousness for the benefit of all. We do this work on behalf of all consciousness. Humility is how we meet our true power.

TO CREATE THAT VISION YOU HOLD IN YOUR HEART, IT IS OK TO SAY NO TO THE ORDINARY.

Are you ready to stop saying yes to an ordinary life? Your intuition is calling you to hear a bigger purpose. It hurts to ignore it, to stay inside the comfort zone of conformity. You are made to be extraordinary.

Ricci–Jane Adams

HOLDING NOTHING BACK. GIVE IT ALL TO THE DIVINE. PRIVILEGE YOUR DEVOTION. IT'S HERE WE CREATE REALITY. HOLD NOTHING BACK FROM GOD.

BE HUMBLED BY YOUR OWN MAGNITUDE.

Why are we not all living lives of absolute bliss, pleasure and peace? Because we don't believe it is possible. We live inside our limits, and we can't outgrow them unless something, usually catastrophic, occurs to smash the limits and show us a new reality. So, we associate growth with sacrifice and struggle. And whilst our evolution does take discipline and devotion, it does not need to be one of constant emotional chaos. At some point, you've got to realise that emotional chaos is a great way to avoid meeting your magnitude. We are all boxed in by our limiting beliefs, no matter how 'woke' we are. There is always more room to take up! We are born for magnitude. Don't believe otherwise.

YOU ARE MADE FOR SO MUCH MORE THAN YOU ARE CURRENTLY ACCEPTING.

Spend time today considering what limits you have accepted that have nothing to do with you. Other people's idea of a good life, for example. What is your measure of your highest possible life? And are you doing what is required to attain it? Or are you sitting inside borrowed limits? We cannot optimise our reality until we know what we are capable of. Is it possible that you've settled? I don't mean in your career, relationship or where you live. I mean in regards to your evolution. Have you spiritually settled? Are you residing inside of a comfort zone with your rituals and devotion but not really expecting that you'll access Infinite consciousness as your normal waking state? Are you using your spiritual devotion to soothe yourself rather than to evolve yourself? Where are you using your tools to bypass your experiences rather than doing the deep work to move yourself through the dark night? Have you become habitual and lazy with your growth, or are you consistently inviting yourself to meet the biggest part of you? Have you settled for a half-arse relationship with God? Get up today or tomorrow, and as you sit on your mat to do your devotion, expect your practice will change your life. That is my intention with everything I undertake, for change is the only indication of spiritual evolution. If you've become stagnant, today is the day to make some change within.

Ricci-Jane Adams

PLEASE PUT DOWN THE LITTLENESS, DEAR BELOVED. WE'VE GOT BIG THINGS TO DO, AND IT'S TIME TO TAKE OFF THE BRAKES.

I'm not referring to your social media list size or monthly revenue. I'm not talking about how much you travel or how many books you've read. I'm speaking to your soul. Are you willing to let the fullness of your truth shine so brightly that the ego fear is silenced? The littleness occurs when we try to deny we are God/dess. Don't deny yourself your truth any longer.

FINALLY, I GET IT. I SURRENDER TO THE BRILLIANCE OF THE DIVINE PLAN FOR MY LIFE. NO MORE HOLDING ONTO MY MEDIOCRE VISION.

We must keep reminding ourselves not to cling to the desires of the ego, its wants and demands based on doubt and fear. We hold so tight to ideas of success, love, power, and happiness that we rob ourselves of truth. We starve the oxygen out of our soul's path. Put it down today. The small, limited vision and open the way to the magnitude of your life's purpose.

Ricci-Jane Adams

NOTHING IS AS IMPORTANT AS OUR THINKING MAKES IT APPEAR.

We tie ourselves in knots. This is not just a turn of phrase. If you could see what happens to your subtle anatomy when you ruminate, obsess, think, and think again, you would know how you literally stop the flow of life force. Instead, hand all the heavy thoughts to God consciousness, aka your higher self and bless them. You'll feel the energy flow return and an ease enter your being. This takes spiritual fierceness because we are all control freaks, and we like to believe we can control the world. Handing over feels like death. But it is a necessary step in our evolution because the illusion of control is our biggest problem on this path of awakening. Surrender. Trust. Understand that in God's hands, nothing is as important as we believe, and everything is already taken care of.

TODAY, RIGHT HERE, RIGHT NOW, I INVITE YOU TO PUT DOWN ANYTHING THAT IS NOT CONGRUENT WITH WHO YOU ARE BECOMING. DON'T BE AFRAID TO DO THE HARD THINGS TO ATTAIN THE FREEDOM YOUR SOUL IS YEARNING FOR. PUT DOWN ALL THE HEAVY, DEAD WEIGHT OF BORROWED BELIEFS AND EMERGE GLORIOUS INTO WHO YOU KNOW YOU ARE.

Ricci–Jane Adams

THE LESS WE BELIEVE THE MORE FREE WE ARE.

Nothing is absolute except for love. The pursuit of truth is ultimately to move beyond man-made belief. When I speak of trinkets and superstitions, I am speaking to all belief. Meaning does not preexist. We assign it individually and collectively. We are the collection of stories we tell about ourselves individually and collectively.

BE SO HUMBLE THAT YOU SHOUT FROM THE ROOFTOPS, UNAFRAID, 'I AM GOD'S GLORIOUS SELF MADE MANIFEST'.

As spiritual seekers, we are not just walking a path that has already been predetermined. We're creating a new paradigm. This is what it is to be that sacred leader, to be unafraid of our holy power. Our responsibility is to know that we are not just walking a path that's already predetermined but that we are generating that path through our grace and humility, through our willingness to be so humble that you shout from the rooftops, *I am God's glorious self-made manifest!*

Ricci–Jane Adams

HERE I STAND, MAKING MY HOME
IN THE UNKNOWN, INVITING
REORIENTATION OF MY BEING SO THAT
A HIGHER ORDER CAN BE BORN FOR ALL.

There will always be a period of disorientation as we move away from the known into the unknown, such as we are experiencing globally at this time. This is what meeting fear is. It is the death of the personality, the little self, to meet who we are beyond our limits. We can use this time to unlearn, mature spiritually, and evolve on behalf of all. This is the path of the sacred seeker.

DEAR GOD,

*I HUMBLY STAND BEFORE THE
SACRED CHAMBER OF MY HEART,
REQUESTING PERMISSION TO ENTER
EVER MORE DEEPLY. I RECOGNISE MY
DESIRE TO HOLD MYSELF BACK FROM
FULLY MERGING WITH THE POWER OF
MY HOLINESS. TODAY, I SURRENDER
TO MYSELF. I AM ALTERED BY THIS
SURRENDER AND MADE MORE HOLY
BY IT. REFINE ME. MAKE ME IN YOUR
IMAGE. LET YOUR GRACE DANCE IN MY
SOUL AND ON MY TONGUE.*

AND SO IT IS. AND IT IS SO.

Ricci-Jane Adams

THERE IS AN ASPECT OF YOU THAT REMAINS UNREALISED. A BOLDER VOICE, A CLEARER VISION, A WILDER KNOWING.

This is good news. There is always more to discover within. There is more to you than even you have realised. Be unrelenting in the pursuit of your glorious truth. This takes unlearning, letting go, and releasing.

WE MUST RECOGNISE THAT WE HEAL THE WORLD BY HEALING OUR SELF-WORTH ISSUES.

Disempowered people create a disempowered world. In your glorious, fierce, holy power, you are the antidote to the suffering world. So give up your addiction to self-loathing, for that is what it is. It is wasted energy. Use that creative heat within you to create gloriousness in the world.

Ricci–Jane Adams

YOU ARE SO WELCOME HERE IN THIS PLACE OF QUIET UNDOING. YOU ARE SAFE TO UNRAVEL AND LET IT ALL GO INTO THE VOID. IT IS HERE THAT LIFE BEGINS.

HOLINESS

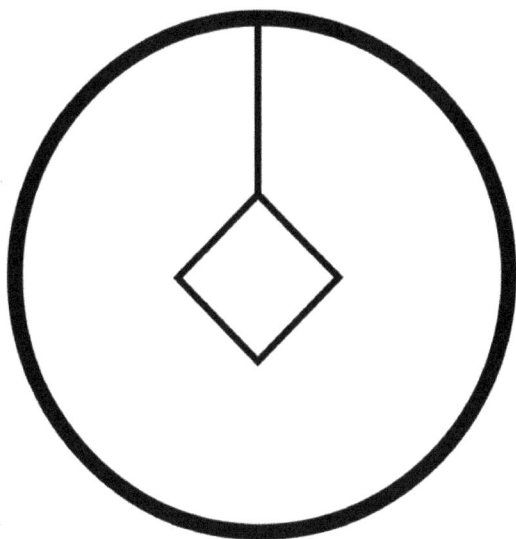

Ricci-Jane Adams

THIS IS YOUR PERMISSION TO DISAPPOINT SOMEONE SO YOU CAN SET YOUR SOUL FREE.

THE PLACE WHERE I STAND IS HOLY GROUND.

What determines your holiness? Your presence in the world. You are the most sacred and divine of all. You are precious beyond measure. You bless everywhere you are with your holiness. And this does not and never can change, regardless of how aware you are of this truth. Nothing you have done or that which has been done to you makes you less sacred. Nothing can increase your holiness, for you are infinite already. But your bliss, your joy, your success, your power? All these things can be increased simply by acknowledging the truth. You make all things holy. I bow to you.

TODAY I LEAD FROM MY HOLINESS.

Our holiness is not conditional. At any moment, we can choose to lead our lives from this state of grace. We can forgive ourselves and others and restore correct perception to see as God/dess sees. Holiness is wholeness. To live holistically is to live from your holiness. It simply requires that your faith and actions are congruent. Be unafraid to let the Infinite lead.

DON'T DOUBT YOURSELF, DEAR ONE. THIS HOLY PATH HAS BEEN HANDMADE FOR YOU, AND YOU WERE BORN READY.

Some days, the task assigned to you by God might feel too big, too awesome, too much for you to carry. Don't try to human it! Lean into your infinite nature.

I AM AN IRRESISTIBLE MAGNET FOR MIRACLES.

This is just the way it is. You ride on the miracle frequency. It takes so much effort to keep rejecting miracles to keep ourselves down. We do it every day. Here we are, bathed in the vibration of miracle upon miracle, turning our hearts away and closing our minds. All it takes is a shift—a shift in perception. Look away from the known into the infinite space of the glorious potential around you. De-identity yourself. Be free to inhabit the miracle. Are you willing to accept the plan God has for your life? This surrender is where the gloriousness kicks in. The unending miracle is the acceptance of what we are. Then, the divine flow of incredible opportunity moves with ease and grace into our lives. I am an irresistible magnet for my truth.

SPIRITUAL ADVENTURE IS MY HIGHEST VALUE. TO JOURNEY INTO THE VAST WILDERNESS OF THE UNIVERSE WITHIN ME, KNOWING THAT I WILL NEVER TIRE OF WHAT I DISCOVER.

I privilege my spiritual life above all else. Spiritual adventure is a daily requirement for me. To go into the world within the world. That is where the adventure takes us. How deep and vast and ancient a journey. Nothing outside of me gives me the same kind of joy.

Ricci-Jane Adams

NOTHING THAT HAPPENS TODAY IS BIGGER THAN MY ABILITY TO CHOOSE WHAT I BELIEVE ABOUT IT.

A miracle is a shift in perception. I can choose which of my thoughts to believe. I can cultivate new thoughts. What power is this! I am the alchemist.

COMPASSION IS SPIRITUAL PERCEPTION. WHEN I PERCEIVE WITH COMPASSION, I SEE YOU AS GOD SEES YOU.

This is compassion. It requires spiritual fierceness to be willing to move beyond the ego-identified self and to align our perception with God consciousness. It requires spiritual maturity, which comes when we choose to privilege our soul nature above all else. This compassion is how we heal ourselves and others. To increase our power to serve, we must choose to go deeper, vaster, and more directly towards our infinite truth.

Ricci-Jane Adams

LET THIS BE YOUR INNER COMPASS TODAY – WHAT DOES MY HOLY HUMAN SELF TRULY DESIRE?

WHEN WE ZOOM OUT AND LOOK AT OUR LIVES FROM THE UNIVERSAL PERSPECTIVE, BEYOND THE HUMAN CHAOS, WE CAN BEGIN TO SEE, EVEN IF WE DO NOT UNDERSTAND HOW THAT OUR AWAKENING IS ALWAYS BEING SERVED.

Ricci-Jane Adams

*CONNECT TO THAT GREATER PART
OF YOU EVERYDAY. SHE IS THERE,
QUIETLY, SOFTLY, TENDERLY WOOING
YOU, ENTICING YOU TO HOLINESS BY
MERGING SELF WITH SELF.*

LET THE SOUL'S AGITATION MOVE YOU. LET IT ALTER YOU. ACCEPT THE HOLY MESSENGER OF YOUR EVOLUTION WITHOUT FEAR. YOU ARE EMERGING, DEAR ONE.

Ricci-Jane Adams

I BOW BEFORE THE TEMPLE OF MY BEING. I AM ALTERED BY REVERENCE FOR MY FIERCE SPIRIT. MY LIFE IS AN OFFERING TO ONENESS. I FALL AT THE FEET OF THE DEPTHS OF MY INTUITIVE KNOWING. I AM THE ORACLE THAT I SEEK.

*YOU'VE GOT EVERYTHING YOU NEED
WITHIN YOU. BUT IT'S YOUR HOLY
RESPONSIBILITY TO LET IT EMERGE
FROM YOU INTO THE WORLD. THIS IS
HOW WE SET OTHERS FREE. THIS IS
HOW WE SAVE THE WORLD.*

Ricci-Jane Adams

BLESS AND PRAY.
SURRENDER AND RELEASE.
REST AND RESET.
BASK AND BATHE.
BREATHE AND FLOW.
COME HOME TO PRESENCE.

A PRAYER FOR THE LOST, AFRAID, GUILTY OR ASHAMED.

The world has not touched you.

Your actions have not diminished you.

Your perfection remains intact in the eyes of the Universe.

You are so worthy.

The Universe will never stop holding you close and whispering to you your life's purpose.

Lean into this warm embrace.

You are unforgiven, for you were never judged.

Your intuition is evidence of your union with the divine.

And it is always there waiting for you to receive.

Ricci–Jane Adams

POWER

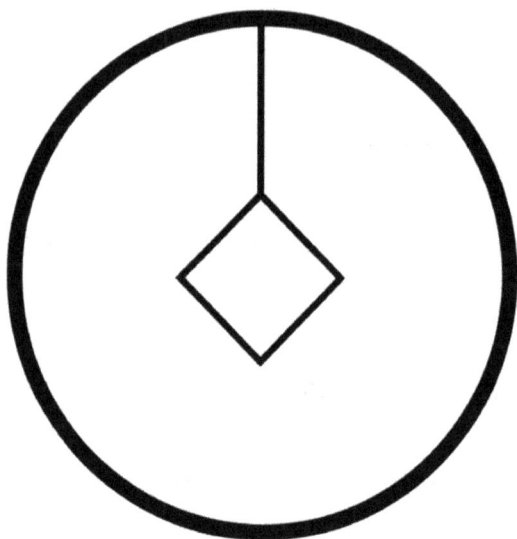

THE ONLY POWER I TRULY POSSESS IS TO KNOW THAT THE POWER I POSSESS IS GOD'S POWER.

Holy power is to know that I am nothing and, paradoxically, everything. I am filled with grace when I humbly accept that I am the Infinite. That's what God feels like. And that grace is a sacred power and moves the world when encountered. It alters people. To be a channel for that graceful power is my service.

Ricci-Jane Adams

YOU WILL FIND ME ONLY IN THE GLORIOUS EMPTINESS BEYOND BELIEF. YOU HAVE NOT MET POWER LIKE MINE BEFORE, A POWER THAT EXISTS BEYOND YOUR IDEAS OF ME.

You have not met me, in truth. You have only met your idea of me. My holy purpose is to become the fullest expression of what I am so that I may burn away all illusions. I am the God/dess made manifest, and when I rise, my light burns so brightly, it is the antidote to the fear through which you see me and the world. I will not be afraid of this task, which is to meet myself as I truly am.

THERE IS SO MUCH POWER IN YOU. NOW IS THE TIME TO SET IT FREE.

You may deeply understand what I'm saying with these words. Or the idea of you being as powerful as the entire Cosmos might feel like a very abstract idea. Either way, what would it take for you today to simply utter this prayer, *Dear God, increase my power to serve*...? Are you willing to meet your sacred power?

Ricci-Jane Adams

ACTIVATING YOUR POWER IS NOT GOING TO WIN YOU FRIENDS AMONGST THOSE WHO ARE IN HIDING FROM THEMSELVES. DO IT ANYWAY.

The spiritual leader has gone further into her divine truth than most. This makes some people uncomfortable. But that's actually the point. To be a demonstration of what is possible for all. The leader is simply saying by their actions, 'Hey, wake up! Look! I've cleared the path for me and you!' For some, that is too much. They'll resist you. They'll fight you. They'll pretend they can't see a path. Don't be deterred, dear Leader. Your example will alter those who are ready.

YOU ARE READY TO STEP INTO YOUR POWER WHEN YOU NO LONGER MEASURE YOUR SUCCESS IN TERMS OF EXTERNAL APPROVAL.

Your power is not your power to be validated by the world. Your power is your willingness to no longer look to the world for validation. We throw the term around loosely, but this is what a thought leader is. Someone who has stepped beyond the world's established ideas to create a new paradigm. You simply cannot do that when you want to be approved of. The sacred leader is in her power because she seeks only to know her worth through her intimacy with the divine. She is self-approving. Withdraw your attention from the external world. Go within and get good with God/dess. When that relationship is primary, you can place your intention on creating whatever you are inspired to create without fear that one disapproving comment will shut you down.

Are you ready? How do we do that when our work is dependent on others 'liking' by investing in us? How do we stay present and in our self-worth when taking our soul and offering it to the world? That's what sacred service is to me. My soul writ large. So, how do I stay true to me? I get good with God. My primary relationship is with God. I have to remember that I trust God. That's how to keep moving forward and keep invested in my creations on this path of sacred service.

I HAVE NEVER LET ANYONE ELSE'S OPINION OF ME BE ANYTHING OTHER THAN FUEL TO FLAME MY FIRE.

Take courage, dear one. Your life is yours to lead. You are sovereign. You are the Queen of your domain. Don't be derailed by other's perceptions. You've got too much amazingness to create today to sit on the sidelines of your life because someone else can't handle your magic. Take back the crown.

Ricci-Jane Adams

YOU'LL SEE SIGNS EVERYWHERE WHEN YOU REALISE YOU CREATE THEM ALL.

Consciousness creates itself. When we understand this, we have to accept that fortune telling, energy forecasting, future predictions, consulting oracle cards, etc., is an act of self-fulfilling prophecy. All that is happening is that the prediction is collapsing the wave function and drawing down that potential from all the trillions of possibilities to make it so. Depending on how much value we place on the predictor, we are more likely to build our reality according to that prediction. We create the signs that we are seeking. That is the power. Be self-sovereigning. Understand the science. Become truly miraculous.

THE MEANING OF SELF-SOVEREIGNTY IS SELF-APPROVAL.

As your power to serve grows, so will the need for you to have your self-worth intact because people will challenge your power, imitate your work, dismiss you, blame you and generally project their unmet fear onto you. This is because the brighter you shine, the more you are a magnet. Yet, those with unhealed pain will want your light, *and* they will want to try to extinguish your light. Be unafraid. No one can diminish you when you have the right relationship with yourself as an infinite and holy power.

Ricci-Jane Adams

IT'S SO MUCH EASIER TO FEEL WORTHLESS AND POWERLESS THAN TO ADMIT THE TRUTH THAT YOU HAVE UNLIMITED HOLY POWER.

Obsession with our littleness keeps us conveniently occupied so we do not meet our holy task: to know ourselves as God. What the world requires to heal all injustice and imbalance is for you to change your mind about yourself and to take inspired action from that higher consciousness. We have always possessed what we need to create heaven on earth. It's as simple as a willingness to look again at yourself with fresh wonder and practise that shift in perception every damn day. If not you, then who?

IT'S NOT THE WEIGHT OF THE LOAD. IT'S THE WAY THAT YOU CARRY IT.

When we're weary in our souls from the world's weight, it's our holy task to rest, not to give up. The weight of the world, whatever that weight is for us, is something we can learn to carry differently. When we lead with our souls, that weight can feel completely different. It's unavoidable that this life will bring some sense of burden. Some days more than others. But privileging our souls will carry us when we can't carry ourselves. It's OK to be tired. It's OK to be heavy. It's OK to rest, and give the soul some space and time. Yet do not be afraid of what you have been tasked to carry by God.

Ricci-Jane Adams

REFINEMENT OF OUR SPIRITUAL NATURE BRINGS A MATURITY OF BEING. WE NO LONGER DEMAND THAT OUR SPIRITUALITY CONSTANTLY PLEASES US.

I AM NOT IN THE UNIVERSE. THE UNIVERSE IS IN ME.

Ricci-Jane Adams

DON'T BE AFRAID OF YOUR EVOLUTION TODAY. CLAIM MORE OF YOURSELF. BE UNAFRAID OF CHANGE.

More often than we realise, we retreat when we meet the full expression of our power and glory. We instinctively know that things will change if we keep moving in that direction that things will change. Relationships will end. You'll have to stop making do with something that doesn't serve you. You might not realise that that is what you are born to do. To evolve into the full expression of what you are - to meet your gloriousness.

THE BEGINNING OF BEING IN YOUR SACRED POWER IS GIVING YOURSELF PERMISSION TO SEE YOURSELF AS SACRED.

Are you willing to acknowledge your preciousness? This is how we fully express what God's consciousness intends for us. This is how we meet our sacred power. Sacred power doesn't denote gentleness, necessarily, although it can. Sacred power can be fierce, fiery, and always fearless.

Ricci-Jane Adams

LEADERSHIP

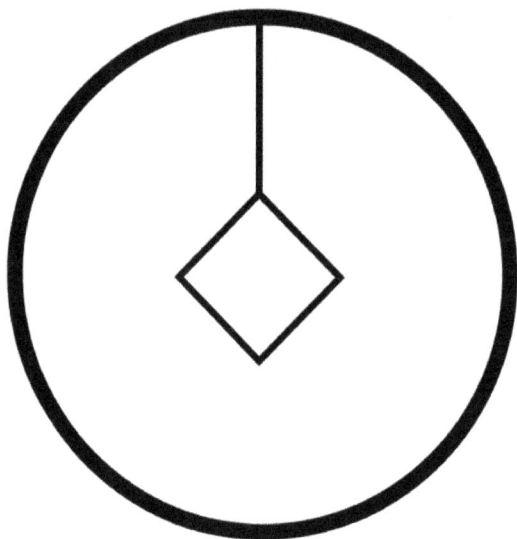

DON'T BE AFRAID OF YOUR SOUL'S PURPOSE. YOU WERE BORN TO MAKE IT HAPPEN.

Most of us don't fear not finding our purpose. We subconsciously fear the discovery of it. Because we are aware deep down in the fabric of our being that when we remember it, we will have to take radical responsibility for our lives. We no longer allow external distractions to take our time in the form of people or events but instead live with single-focused sight and profound commitment. Every breath is an opportunity to get closer to our truth. This is what it feels like to live a purpose-led life. Optimised, radicalised, no longer seeking the mundane comforts but willingly walking off the path of the known to break new ground.

Ricci-Jane Adams

A LEADER HAS SIMPLY TAUGHT HERSELF TO GET OVER HERSELF AND GET ON WITH THE WORK OF PARADIGM CHANGE.

The Leader's Manifesto.

We stand for sacred service at the core of all that we do. We know that we do not do this work for ourselves alone and that our commitment to walk this path congruently is the medicine for all, including ourselves. We do not pursue our path of sacred service for personal gain or the attainment of the betterment of our own lives alone. Our work is in the world on behalf of all.

We understand our privilege and freedom in pursuing our soul's awakening and will not squander that privilege. It is our privilege to be of service, and we know it has nothing to do with our personal (personality) agenda. We are God's hands and feet in the world, and we take our instructions directly from the Source, even when inconvenient and uncomfortable. We are not here for our comfort but for our evolution.

*DO NOT BE AFRAID OF YOUR POWER,
EVEN IF IT MAKES OTHERS WHO ARE
USED TO SEEING YOU PLAY SMALL AS
UNCOMFORTABLE AS HELL.*

I WILL MEET MYSELF AS GOD/DESS. ENOUGH WITH THE LITTLENESS.

Sacred leaders are not particularly 'special'. But they are extraordinary. They are not necessarily born leaders or the gifted few. What makes them extraordinary is not their talents, modalities or skills. Only their willingness to descend into their underworld and meet their innate holiness makes these people such glorious demonstrations of the true power of God/dess. Each one of them learns how to serve at the will of God/dess, consecrating all that they do, setting their ego desires aside, and instead of pandering to the addictions of fear, they go within and sit face to face with it. Right up close and cosy. They hunt down that fear through their devotional practices, for it can show them exactly where their work lies. They have learnt to hold their own container and be their own guide. They are fully human yet fully divine.

LITTLENESS IS NOT ABOUT WHAT WE DO BUT OUR PERCEPTION OF OURSELVES. IF WE ARE WILLING TO CHANGE OUR MINDS ABOUT WHAT WE ARE, OUR ROLE IN AWAKENING PLANETARY CONSCIOUSNESS WILL CHANGE. NO MORE WITH THE LITTLENESS. IT IS AN ADDICTION. WE MUST MEET OURSELVES AS GOD/DESS THROUGH SILENCE, STILLNESS AND SOLITUDE. OUR DEVOTION LEADS THE WAY.

Ricci-Jane Adams

ALL THE GREAT SPIRITUAL LEADERS ARE SPIRITUAL REBELS/ REVOLUTIONARIES.

All of us who are born free enough must do the work of dismantling a reality that keeps some enslaved whilst others benefit. This is what Jesus did. His spiritual path was radical service. It's time we take his lead. All the great spiritual avatars were spiritual rebels/revolutionaries. They strove to end systems of hate and oppression because that's what you do when you wake up and truly awaken. You're not here to get more for your reality. You're here to lead at this most extraordinary time. If your vision board doesn't include liberation for all, you need to revise your vision.

IF YOUR SOUL SHAKES WITH PURPOSE AND YOUR WISDOM IS BURNING TO BE HEARD, THEN RISE TO YOUR FEET AND SHARE IT.

Stand at the front of the room, the top of the mountain, on the stage, in the boardroom, in the community centre, and let your voice be heard. We have been silenced for thousands of years. Don't accept the idea that to be a spiritual woman in her power, you must resist your desire to lead. Rise to your feet and lead the revolution.

Every woman who can lead must. This is not the time to turn ourselves away, to wrap ourselves in knots, to be concerned with being well-liked and approved of, or to make others comfortable. Do not sit inside your fear of being seen as though that is humility. The spiritual leader must become humility itself if she is to lead powerfully, but humility is not what we think it is. It has nothing to do with rejecting our power and everything to do with knowing that our power is the power of the Infinite moving through us. We can, of our own selves, do nothing. We are

263

here in service to our souls. God's power is our power.

This is humility, not some false modesty that means you dull your shine, resist your voice, sit passively when you should be unafraid to say, 'This is what I am. I know this by God's grace, and I am ready to speak'. If you are, dear sister, drawn to lead, then the world will get uncomfortable with you. It will ask you to sit down, fit in, and quiet yourself down. How can you be so self-approving that the opinion of a domesticated, dulled, and disenfranchised world will not matter?

How can you become self-sovereigning? This is the true quest of the divine feminine now. For, in becoming that, you lend that power to all women who are not yet awakened to their truth. Teaching is demonstrating. Be the demonstration of a woman unafraid to be ALL that she is.

IT TAKES SO MUCH COURAGE TO WALK THIS PATH, DEAR ONE. I SEE YOU. I HONOUR YOUR FIERCE SOUL, WAKING UP IN A SLEEPING WORLD.

Being the spiritual leader takes so much revolutionary heat. It takes connection and community and gathering together. It takes, also, stillness, solitude and silence. This takes more courage. To sit alone before God/dess unafraid to look into the face of the Infinite and know it is your reflection looking back at you. Are you ready to sit with God? Are you prepared to meet yourself? Are you willing to put down the trinkets, superstitions, noise, and doubt to do without others approval?

Yes, you are. The world is waiting.

Ricci-Jane Adams

I CHOOSE TODAY TO BE UNAFRAID OF MY POWER.

It sounds like a straightforward statement. But we feel in our bones that there is danger in the idea of power. We feel the weight of history upon us. We feel the deep wound of patriarchal power inside our guts, cells, and veins. What do we do with the responsibility of power when so many have failed before us? We recognise the truth. Our only power is to know that our power is the power of God/dess. In this, we serve through our power. We are unafraid.

IT IS NOT UNTIL WE EXPERIENCE OURSELVES AS GOD/DESS THAT WE CAN LEAD FROM THAT PARADIGM.

When we choose to lead, we choose to meet ourselves as God. When we meet ourselves as God, our vision will become as glorious as we are. When we permanently shift from fear to love, we want nothing from the world. What could we meet in the dream of separation that is a match for meeting ourselves in unity and Oneness? To be God's grace in the world will be all that we desire so that others may meet themselves as that. People will look and say, 'Your life is a miracle. You have everything. You are so successful'. And you will laugh and know that the richness is within.

Ricci–Jane Adams

SACRED LEADERSHIP IS THE DIVINE RESPONSIBILITY TO LEAD OURSELVES TO THE TRUTH OF WHAT WE ARE.

Sacred leadership is always self-leadership, for it demonstrates our congruence between faith and actions to the world. This is how we lead from our divinity.

BE MORE FAITHFUL TO YOURSELF THAN ANYONE ELSE.

How many times a day do you betray yourself to keep others happy or even to prevent yourself from moving towards your own dreams? Putting yourself last is an addiction to staying small and letting other people's lives be more valuable. It's simply not possible to live this way because ALL IS ONE. How you treat yourself is how you treat others. Think deeply about this. Moving in the direction of your intuition is to move towards deep self-respect. What would it take for you to privilege your own needs truly?

YOUR TRUTH IS A MAGNETIC FORCE THAT WON'T REST UNTIL IT FINDS YOU.

Know thyself is the most potent spiritual edict there is. We want to rush the process. Mostly, we are impatient and want to be able to claim who we are right away. But here's the thing. Your truth is the same as it is for all. You are pure, unlimited consciousness. You are God. Your life's work is to find your way back to that truth and be a living demonstration of it. You'll know you're on the right path when your life feels joyful. The path will keep getting deeper and richer as you journey. You'll know yourself increasingly with every step, so don't proclaim your identity too quickly. For here is the delicious paradox. The closer you come to your God nature, the less you identify with categories, forms, and ideas of the world. You recognise yourself in everything. You realise you are that. It is a beautiful path. Take your time. Enjoy it. The journey is the destination. And the less you attach to identity, the faster your truth will find you.

Make a vessel of yourself. Be empty enough to recognise your truth when it finds you. Empty enough to hear above the noise and chaos of life. If you are already full of ideas of who you are, then there is no space for the higher truth. Empty yourself out. Believe less. Make space for the Infinite.

PLEASE STOP BEING AFRAID OF YOUR OWN GLORIOUS SELF.

We are made to be glorious and have dumbed ourselves down to keep ourselves and anyone else comfortable. Consciously, you might agree, but undoubtedly, there is a subconscious program that says it is downright dangerous to be the full expression of what you are. You'll be rejected by the pack, the family, and the community. Deep, ancient programs that make us fear for our lives, all those lifetimes we lost our lives for being different to expectations. It's not that time anymore, dear one. And your most outstanding service is fully expressing infinite consciousness in the world. You are God consciousness made manifest. Let your life be an expression of God's glory.

SACRED LEADERSHIP IS SEEING GOD IN ANOTHER EVEN WHEN THEY CANNOT SEE GOD IN YOU.

Ricci-Jane Adams

THERE IS A CERTAIN IRRESISTIBLE GLOW ABOUT THE WOMAN WHO IS LEADER OF HER OWN LIFE.

I see so many women attain this glow when they begin to recognise how little the vision they held for themselves was. As they start to emerge, the flush of Infinite, holy power overtakes them. This is the glow—recognition of the glorious power to lead their lives.

THE SACRED LEADER DOES NOT RESIDE IN THE COMFORT ZONE. SHE LEADS BECAUSE SHE IS A VISIONARY AND CAN SEE WHAT OTHERS CANNOT YET SEE.

Don't be afraid of leaving your comfort zone, dear leader. You were born to do this. Show the world who you are.

Ricci–Jane Adams

*WE'RE DONE WITH THE WORLD
HEALER IN THE NEW PARADIGM. I AM
ONLY INTERESTED IN SACRED
LEADERS. LEAD ME TO MY HOLINESS,
AND MY HEALING IS INEVITABLE.*

WE ARE READY TO EMBODY THE SACRED LEADER WHEN WE ARE READY TO PRIVILEGE OUR INNER WORLD BEFORE ALL ELSE.

What differentiates sacred leadership from any other kind of leadership? The sacred leader does her primary work on the energetic plane. She is not interested in commanding matter. She learns to dance with frequency for the benefit of all. She is here in sacred service and unafraid to lead the creation of a new paradigm for all. She privileges the deep work, the inner realms, and the world within the world, for this is how she creates change at the level of the gross material plane.

Ricci–Jane Adams

*SACRED LEADERSHIP IS NOT
SOMETHING WE DO. IT IS A STATE OF
BEING CREATED BY DEVOTION. THE
SACRED LEADER IS CONGRUENT
BETWEEN HER FAITH AND HER
ACTIONS IN THE WORLD.*

The sacred leader is easily identified. She is the one living her truth. Don't be impressed by words. Look to deeds and actions. Congruence created by devotion is the mark of the sacred leader. It is a state of being we are all born to inhabit, but not all will. It takes courage, soul fire, humility and the willingness to accept our power. This is our willingness to accept ourselves as God/dess. Sacred leadership is to be the fullest demonstration of what you are. In other words, to inhabit yourself as God. What do we do with that responsibility? How do we work with this deep soul calling that is often so terrifying? Our commitment is to remember that we do not awaken for ourselves alone.

THE SACRED LEADER IS NOT INTERESTED IN YOUR COMFORT BUT YOUR EVOLUTION.

The sacred leader is the archetype of our age. Our spiritual awakening must charge us with the responsibility to take that path out in service to the greater good. How do you tell when you're working with a sacred leader? She holds the space for your brilliance, which sounds great. And it is. Except be prepared. She is not interested in your littleness. She is interested in your evolution. She won't hold space for the broken-down vision of yourself. She sees who you truly are and creates space for your truth. That doesn't always make her popular. But this isn't a popularity competition. This is the work of our lives. Be the leader. Turn your seeking into leadership.

Ricci-Jane Adams

THE SACRED LEADER IS UNAFRAID TO GO WHERE OTHERS HAVE NOT YET GONE.

Your life is calling you, always, into the unknown. This is evolution. The spiritual leader is the one who does not say no to this call. She is unafraid to exist beyond other people's ideas of the world to lead a new paradigm for all.

TO BE THE SACRED LEADER IS TO BRING THE QUALITIES OF THE SACRED TO ANY SITUATION YOU ARE IN.

New paradigm leadership isn't about what you do or having a platform. It's about congruence. Can you bring the sacred to everyone and everything in your life, especially when it is challenging? It is easy to be the sacred leader when everyone is watching. What about when no one is?

TO LEAD MEANS TO BE THE DEMONSTRATION OF YOUR FAITH.

There's a new paradigm of consciousness pulsating its way into reality. Beyond the trinkets and superstitions of the new age, it demands our congruence. To heal is to create the space for the magnificence of the other and to let them lead themselves to their healing, whatever that may be. To call yourself a healer in this new paradigm is a risky business, for in the age of sovereignty, you better be very clear your role as a healer is to serve others to meet the leader within them and not just give them temporary relief from symptoms. It's much more significant work. It is the work of our time.

THE SPIRITUAL PATH IS NEVER ONE THAT HAPPENS IN ISOLATION. OUR CONSCIOUSNESS IS INHERENTLY INTERCONNECTED.

The aware and prepared sacred leader knows that what she offers to herself, she offers to all. Her path is not for her gain but for the ease of the collective suffering. It is a divine responsibility. If you have the privilege and the freedom to pursue your spiritual awakening, then your question must always be, *how may I be of service*? It violates the cosmic laws to attain spiritual knowledge and to do nothing but hoard it for yourself. Sacred leadership is about holy service. And you were born to do it.

THIS IS TRUE LEADERSHIP. TO BE WILLING AND UNAFRAID TO SAY, 'YES, I WILL DEVOTE MYSELF TO MEET MY FEAR EVERY DAMN DAY'.

Fear is the messenger. Listen deeply. Anger is fear. Rage is fear. Injustice is fear. Stress is fear. Anxiety is fear. Hopelessness is fear. Let it alter you. Listen to it. It's guiding you home. Fear is not the problem. Let it have its way with you. It is here to correct the error. If something is wrong, listen. You're being called back to truth. But you must sit in the fire of your fear. You must walk through it. There is no going around this. Where am I in denial? Where must I correct the error? Be with the fear. Let it move to you to evolve. Don't bypass it. Don't numb it. Let it be your teacher. This is the shadow work. *What have I been holding within me that goes against my truth?* Seek it out. Witness it. This is the healing, individually and collectively. It is our divine responsibility.

I SEE YOU, DEAR ONE. HAVE THE COURAGE TODAY. STAY AWAY FROM WANTING AN ORDINARY LIFE. YOU'RE INVITED TO CHANGE THE WORLD. STAY TRUE.

To all my leaders, teachers, mentors, guides, revolutionaries, game changers, soul shakers and paradigm busters, today is yours. Stay away from the ordinary, normal, nice, and acceptable. Shake the spiritual tree. Honour your unshakable faith. Be comfortable with being unacceptable. Make waves. Make love. Make today your masterpiece.

Ricci-Jane Adams

INCREASING OUR POWER TO SERVE MEANS OVERCOMING IDENTIFICATION WITH EGO-SELF AND ESTABLISHING A DEEP SPIRITUAL INTIMACY. TRUE SELF-ESTEEM IS ABOUT GETTING OVER OURSELVES.

EPILOGUE

Go at this thing called life with arms and eyes wide open.

Let fear motivate you, not hinder you.

Give yourself over to wonder.

Let life crack your heart wide open.

Don't be afraid of the exquisite pain of loving.

Know your worth. You are infinite and unlimited and then dare to live that way.

Be the demonstration of your faith.

Question everything.

Keep evolving and don't settle.

Be curious, not defensive and wildly generous.

Take the action required in any given situation.

Don't let your history determine your future.

Love easily but know when to walk away.

Don't be cynical. Be wonder-full.

Everything is amazing and hard and glorious and ugly, and it all exists to show us the way home to truth.

Become intimate with your spiritual nature.

Bow down to this crazy, precious life every day.

See how much good you can do with it.

ABOUT THE INSTITUTE
FOR INTUITIVE INTELLIGENCE

We lead the revolution in the intuitive sciences and sacred leadership by providing access to world-class, socially responsible, ethical and trauma informed evidence-based training programs. The Institute has pioneered a revolutionary approach to training intuition and is committed to creating a gold-standard benchmark in the field of the intuitive sciences because, in an unregulated industry, the standards we set are our own. Excellence, ethical service, the pursuit of spiritual innovation and ongoing research inform all of the activities of the Institute, for this is how we can take the new conversation on intuition to the world.

Learn more about the Institute's programs here instituteforintuitiveintelligence.com/

ABOUT DR RICCI-JANE ADAMS

Hey, hey beloved, I'm Ricci-Jane. A researcher, writer and intuition geek dedicated to elevating your intuition to the level of superconsciousness. I have never doubted that I had a tremendous purpose in this life. Raised in a spiritual home, the path of awakening was always my passion, and I sensed that my work in the world would emerge from this passion even as a child. In 2014, with twenty plus years of intuition exploration under my belt, I was yearning to go even deeper. I wanted a university-style qualification that brought with it a community of like-minded, equally devoted and geeky intuitives. No matter where I looked, and boy did I look, I couldn't find it. I knew I had to make it. And that's what I did.

From Reiki, to dramatherapy, to theatre studies, to playwriting, to Transpersonal Counselling, and eventually even to completing a doctorate in magical realism at the University of Melbourne, seeking to know more, to become more, to understand more is at the very heart of me. Every path I have taken has always been informed by a desire to know my soul nature more intimately. What I came back to time and again was intuition. Of course, it was! Intuition is the language of the Cosmos. It is how we connect our human reality with our divine truth. It is everything.

Love Notes to the Divine

As a researcher by trade, I set about learning everything I could about intuition. But so much of what I found left me wanting. Built on the trinkets and superstitions of the new age, many of the teachings were superficial or asked me to give my power to crystals or oracle cards, or worse to a psychic or healer. I knew undoubtedly this is our greatest spiritual skill, so why was it being shared in such a way? Intuition is the language of the cosmos. It is how we connect our human reality with our divine truth. It is everything.

I have spent the last 30 years on a quest to know the truth about intuition – how it works, what it is, where it emerges from, why it works, and even when it works! What I uncovered in researching and living and teaching all that I was learning is a revolutionary method to increasing our innate intuition that has never failed. It is a method of turning on our intuition to become a state of being, not something that we tune in and out of. My vision became so very clear. To train an extraordinary collective to take their intuition to the level of spiritual superpower so that they can support others to increase their connection to their own deepest states of intuition. Intuitive Intelligence® guides us home to the truth that we are unlimited. The Institute was created to show you how.

Learn more about Ricci-Jane Adams here

www.riccijaneadams.com

www.ingramcontent.com/pod-product-compliance
Lightning Source LLC
Chambersburg PA
CBHW071849090426
42811CB00004B/542